MW00397889

don't forget to
dream

don't forget to
dream

pursuing a life that matters—shaped by the heart of God

TIM DOWDY
WITH TIM LUKE

BETHANYHOUSE
MINNEAPOLIS, MINNESOTA

Published by Bethany House Publishers
11400 Hampshire Avenue South
Bloomington, Minnesota 55438

Bethany House Publishers is a division of
Baker Publishing Group, Grand Rapids, Michigan.

Printed in the United States of America

In keeping with biblical principles of creation stewardship, Baker Publishing Group advocates the responsible use of our natural resources. As a member of the Green Press Initiative, our company uses recycled paper when possible. The text paper of this book is comprised of 30% post-consumer waste.

Library of Congress Cataloging-in-Publication Data

Dowdy, Tim P.
  Don't forget to dream : pursuing a life that matters—shaped by the heart of God/ Tim P. Dowdy with Tim Luke.
      p.   cm.
  Summary: "Inspiration for young adults to pursue the only dream worth living—a lifetime shaped by the heart of God—through five major areas: Decisions, Relationships, Enthusiasm, Aspirations, and Mission. You live the dream when you begin to live as the person God made you to be"—Provided by publisher.
  ISBN-13: 978-0-7642-0410-4 (pbk.)
  ISBN-10: 0-7642-0410-6 (pbk.)
  1. Young adults—Religious life. 2. Young adults—Conduct of life.
3. Dreams—Religious aspects—Christianity. I. Luke, Tim. II. Title.
  BV4529.2.D69   2007
  248.8'3—dc22   2007002597

contents

Right Where You Are

Before most of you had ever heard of Casting Crowns, Tim Dowdy was my pastor. I still serve under him as one of the student pastors at Eagle's Landing First Baptist Church, and I see young people every day who can benefit from the truths recorded in these pages.

I see the aimlessness to which Pastor Tim speaks in this book, but I also see its source.

As a young adult, you often feel like people are telling you what to do, but you're afraid that if you respond, it won't be good enough—so why try? It's like the bar is set too high, and so many young people are convinced they can't be all that their parents, teachers, and coaches are telling them. Many parents come at their children with a "you're-the-hope-of-the-world" bit that kids don't want to hear. You're like, "Dude, I'm failing math and my girlfriend broke up with me. I don't want to be the hope of the world. I can't figure out my own life." The concept is so abstract that it doesn't make sense when people start saying, "You're the hope of the future. You're the church of tomorrow."

At the same time, life grows a bit strange when you become a young adult. When you're a teenager, you have grown sick of being told what to do. Yet when you're suddenly eighteen, you gaze into an uncertain tomorrow, swallow hard, and whisper to yourself, "Would someone just please tell me what to do?" But there's a catch-22 because it's almost impossible to admit that. It's easier to shift into denial and wade into a prolonged sabbatical of figuring yourself out through your late teens and early twenties.

If I've struck a nerve, it's because I've lived it. It is ironic that both Pastor Tim and I were called into the ministry as young adults who were wondering what to do with their lives. I appreciate his interest in young people, and I can tell you from personal experience that it is genuine. I also appreciate his approach in this book.

It is refreshing that, while he has been a successful pastor, he takes us back to a time when he was as clueless as the next guy. He doesn't spare himself in this book, which is a rare quality. Anytime somebody successful starts talking, many young people automatically tune them out as if they see that person as some sort of superhero with a cape. The teenager or young adult believes he never, ever could be that person. And we're that way with God's Word. We read about Paul and think Paul was a super-Christian and was a member of the Jesus X-Men or something. We think, *On my best day, maybe I could be a friend of Paul's, but I could never be Paul.* So when a person who has actually succeeded writes a book, we tend to think, *Yeah, but that's you. I'm me, and you don't know me.* So when Pastor Tim talks about working at

McDonald's and flipping burgers, he starts speaking to us on our level.

Pastor Tim takes what God's Word says about all of us—not what God's Word says about preachers—and shares principles that work for farmers, dentists, stay-at-home moms, teachers—everybody. He uses Scripture to create a level playing field.

He puts himself right where you are. Because he's been there . . . right where you are.

God obviously has a plan for us, and the cool thing is that He has designed us specifically for it. We were made for it. We have all of the natural gifts, the personality traits, the spiritual gifts, and the talents for it. The way we are, the way we think, the way we see life—everything is put into us specifically for the purpose and mission God has for us.

And here He is trying to sell us on it.

That's the weirdest thing in the world when you think about it. God has to sell us on what we're created to do, and we're out here trying to be square pegs in round holes. Part of the reason He has to sell us on it is because of our fear. I think we're all afraid that He's going to send us to Africa or something—which, now that I've traveled there to perform, I wouldn't mind. But we're all afraid He's going to do something crazy with our lives, and we act like He really isn't thinking of us. Our lack of trust is exposed.

Pastor Tim reminds you that God really does know what He has for you because He made you for it. I believe that you are never more happy than when you know you are doing what you were created to do. Being in Casting Crowns didn't make me complete. I've known for years that serving as a youth pastor is my calling. It's what I'm supposed to do. Singing is great, but a record company telling me that I'm significant doesn't make me significant. I knew we were reaching people long before we signed a record deal.

Not everyone grasps this truth. Our preconceived notions about the future can get really messed up sometimes. We think everything depends on us and we're going to blow it if we're not careful. I guess the big realization comes when we start to understand that God is not hiding from us. It's not like He's constructed a big riddle that we're supposed to solve to be successful.

Instead, He lovingly answers your silent cries with His own whisper: "If you'll just trust me and follow me—right now in this very next thing I'm saying—then I'll show you the next step. In fact, I'll do it every time. And I'll be right there with you . . . right where you are."

Love Them Like Jesus,

Mark Hall
Casting Crowns

Spring had sprung in my waning days of high school, the vitality and zeal of new life buzzing every-where but in my heart. For me, it was the same old, same old. My dreams of a future in basketball had wilted in the winter's freeze and, if they had ever been there at all, my determination and ambition for the proverbial "bright future" hadn't survived the thaw.

My grades were horrible. My SAT score laughable. I worked at McDonald's, for goodness' sake. . . .

I had no stinkin' clue what I was going to do with my life.

I was supposed to go to college. I realized that. Isn't that what everyone is supposed to do? It's on the flip side of the Ten Commandments tablets, I suppose: Go to high school, work hard, graduate, go to college, promptly choose a major that locks you in for the rest of your life, work hard, graduate, get a job, be diligent (and loyal), work hard, buy some comfortable brown shoes, work harder, retire, die shortly after retirement, and then have everyone talk about how not working anymore killed you.

Oh, joy.

I thought about it and thought about it. One day, I gurgled almost in despair: *"I really don't know what I'm going to do or where I'm going to go."*

It weighed on my eighteen-year-old psyche like too many eggs in one basket. This hotshot high-school hoopster had zero prospects to pursue my passion beyond North Clayton High School in Riverdale, Georgia. College programs tend to shy away from six-foot-two point guards with a barely above-average shot, little quickness, and just enough fast-twitch muscle fiber to flip a Quarter Pounder.

I still had no stinkin' clue what I was going to do with my life.

So I planned to use college as a stall tactic. I was *supposed* to go anyway, so I decided to enroll, go to a few classes, and dive into Life 101 later. Much later. At first I didn't know if I could even get into college. Ultimately, my dad would have to convince the college president to give me a shot, which he did . . . as long as I understood that I was on academic probation when I first darkened the door. My less-than-spectacular grades and SAT score left me with little margin for error.

Before I graduated high school, my mom saw me moping through another aimless, befuddled day.

"I can tell this is really bothering you," she said. "Let me ask you a question: Have you prayed about it?"

"No, I haven't prayed about it," I said. "This is *my* life, and I want to choose something I want to do."

"Well, honey, did you ever think that God is the one who made you, and He has a plan for your life?"

I was eighteen and smarted off. My parents were the faithful ones. They had dragged me through the church doors three times a week, so I was often there more in body than in spirit.

"Well, I really don't care," I said. "I have my own life to plan."

After a couple days, Mom's words and God's Spirit began to gnaw at my self-will. I had no idea what would come next in my life, but I was scared to admit it to myself and embarrassed to admit it to others.

All I could think was, *I'm about to graduate, and I'm going to have some loser job for the rest of my life.* I wanted more, but I didn't know what to do.

My room was upstairs in our little split-level home. I remember sitting there one day as Mom's words ricocheted through the chambers of my heart. *"Have you prayed about it?"* I was a believer. Seven years earlier, a hippie-looking counselor at a Royal Ambassadors camp in Panama City Beach, Florida, had led me to the Lord. But I wasn't exactly a spiritual giant. I didn't walk daily with God, and I didn't know His heart. Finally, I caved.

Looking back, I know who was cranking the winepress.

So I prayed. It was deep. Profound. It rattled the windows of heaven. It went something like this:

"Okay, God, if you happen to have an idea about what I'm supposed to be doing, I wish you would tell me."

Amen.

And amen.

At the time, I had a 1972 Chevelle and hair that reached my shoulders and was parted down the middle. I was a happening little dude. I prayed that ridiculous prayer, got up, and went to work. My McDonald's-issue attire fit my mood of that entire era.

Blue.

I got off work late because I helped close down the restaurant, and everyone was sound asleep when I got home, but the television was on downstairs. That was very unusual. My parents were disciplined people. They never left the television playing.

I remember walking in, setting down my keys, and looking around to see who must have been awake after midnight. But no one was up. I was alone. Or at least I thought I was.

A Billy Graham crusade was on TV. I have no idea the locale of the crusade. I never would have watched such a program, but when I turned toward the television, the first words out of his mouth asked this question:

"Do you know what God wants you to do with your life?"

I smarted off at him too. Audibly, I answered, "No, but I wish He would tell me."

I had prayed my prayer of the ages that afternoon. And now God was asking me questions through Billy Graham. I reached to change channels but paused. I sat on the couch and listened. I wasn't sure why, but I listened. I probably made it through about half of his sermon before growing groggy and deciding to head to bed, but his message pounded one thought into my heart: "God has a plan for your life. You need to live according to God's plan. There is no better place to live."

When I finally turned off the TV, I thought, *Well, I don't know what that plan is.*

I began climbing the stairs to my bedroom when it happened.

In my heart there was an explosion, one that would change my life from that moment forward. Somewhere between the bottom of the stairs and the doorknob to my bedroom, I learned what I was supposed to do with my life.

On the spot, God answered my prayer from the previous afternoon. I know what I heard. To this day, there is no doubt in my mind.

I raced back downstairs to make sure I had not heard Billy Graham again—to make sure I had turned off the TV.

But the TV was off.

There was a little blue dot in the middle of a black screen. . . .

Having Your Being

Do you still hope?

Do you still dream?

I'm referring to life dreams—plans, aspirations, and goals that are full of purpose, ambition, and adventure. It seems as if many people, everyday folks like you and me, have given up hope and given in to disenchantment because they're so used to their dreams not turning out as they expected or ending in failure. There seems to be a sense of simmering unrest in the souls of many, but there need not be.

I believe that God has a specific dream for every person, and He longs to see you grab it, absorb it, breathe it, live it. And I believe He'll move heaven and earth to help you.

I hope you will allow me to pull up a chair and share with you many lessons I have learned through hard knocks that I want to help you avoid. God has given me the awesome and unique privilege of spending a lot of time around exciting young people. Not only do I pastor Eagle's Landing First Baptist Church in McDonough, Georgia, but I also serve as president of the board of Eagle's Landing Christian Academy, which has more than thirteen hundred students. I have a front-row view of the social and spiritual lives of young adults just like you. I am also raising one. My son, Micah, was in our academy's graduating class of 2006.

Our school produces many fine students, the vast majority of whom go on to attend college. Others dive right into the workplace. In some I see excellence and virtue. In some I sense passion and determination. Yet in some I sense something else—something that blows the dust off the memories of my own young adult life and stirs my heart to want to help.

What is it?

I can only explain it as a sense of feeling lost. I know the feeling well. First come questions like, "What are you going to do with your life?" They're usually followed only by a shrug of the shoulders. Or maybe silence and a deep stare into a murky tomorrow.

It is a tough place to exist, knowing that you have only one life to live but not knowing how you are supposed to live it.

I've watched kids excel through four years of high school only to join the carefree caravan and pull over into a rest stop paved with little initiative and even less conviction. It is an age-old dilemma that I believe has worsened within the past decade.

Some cases are hard core. Others are less severe. After all, it is normal to spar with uncertainty in those young adult years in which independence—glorious independence!—is at once exhilarating and somewhat frightening. Wherever you are in this difficult journey called adulthood, don't despair.

You can live the dream just like anyone else.

I know what it means to wonder . . . and to wander. I know what it's like to be scared. So I'd like to share from personal experience the five major areas through which God has worked to help me live the dream He has for me. They emerge in the acrostic D-R-E-A-M:

- **Decisions**
- **Relationships**
- **Enthusiasm**
- **Aspirations**
- **Mission**

In these pages, you will discover hope and the reason for your hope—the reason that you can trust the following truth:

The only dream worth living is not a nighttime journey into the Land of Nod.

Nor is it a daytime drift into a tomorrow that will never be.

It is neither fantasy nor folly.

Instead, the only dream worth living is infinitely more simple. It is . . .

a lifetime shaped by the heart of God.

I'm not talking about imagining you're some big shot reaching for the stars. I'm talking about realizing that the One who named each and every star did it because He first had you in mind. I'm talking about realizing that you're already an unspeakably wonderful creation who is part of something greater than even you are. I'm talking about grasping the eternal truth that your life *does matter*.

You are made by God. You are made for God. You are uniquely designed. And you begin to live a dream—to live *the* dream—when you live as the person God made you to be.

This book contains one section for each of the five major areas—Decisions, Relationships, Enthusiasm, Aspirations, and Mission. Within each section are three short chapters:

- **Remember** (anecdotes from my experiences in each of these critical areas)
- **Remind** (principles and encouragement for your journey)
- **Resolve** (a DREAM challenge to help you firm up your intentions in each area)

I don't have all the answers. But I do have one. This I offer you.

Curious? Are you truly ready to hear it? You may be tempted to shrug it off now, but just know that the universe was established to point you to this one—and only one—answer:

God made you to enjoy a relationship with Him and to fulfill His plans and purpose for your life.

That's it. That's the answer. It's the only way you'll ever be fulfilled. It's the only map to true joy and contentment. It's the only authentic dream to live.

If you could find a road map that outlined the course to a fulfilling and rewarding life, would you use it?

Well, there is one. I promise.

The Bible is the blueprint for the dream. If you're skeptical, I ask you to set aside any preconceived notions and give God a chance.

For instance, let me share a snippet of how the Bible points us to abundant life. In Acts 17:22–28, the apostle Paul is standing on Mars Hill in Athens, Greece, and addressing philosophers who love to debate about various religions. They are so open to any belief—and are so intent on covering all options—that they have erected an altar with this generic inscription: "TO AN UNKNOWN GOD."

Paul sets the record straight. He says, "Now what you worship as something unknown I am going to proclaim to you." He goes on to tell them about the one true God, the dream-fulfilling God who "determined the times set for" all men and "the exact places where they should live."

Paul explains that God did this "so that men would seek him and perhaps reach out for him and find him." Then he provides the most telling nugget of all:

For in him we live and move and have our being. (Acts 17:28)

In God we live and move and have our being.

What an awesome verse to remind you that the dream already has been provided. You don't have to dream it up. God already has dreamed it for you—and wait till you get a load of His imagination. You have the privilege of living out the dream (having your being) before Him.

That requires a few words that leave us uncomfortable—trust, sacrifice, and obedience—but they truly are the keys to a fulfilled life.

Don't ask, "What am I going to *do*?" Rather, you should ask, "Who am I going to *be*?" The doing will take care of itself if you recognize that in God you truly live, move, and have your being.

You may accept this truth and wonder how to respond. How do you live the dream? What are the steps to walking in God's light instead of straining to see life as if through the dim, amber haze of the alarm clock that beckons a new day?

Let's find out together.

I dare you to continue reading and respond to the forthcoming challenges. I dare you to take God up on His Word—to live and move and have your being *in Him*.

I dare you to see what happens when you take a U-turn away from the carefree caravan and genuinely accept the greatest encouragement I can offer:

Don't forget to DREAM!

decisions

I once had the privilege of playing basketball against Magic Johnson, Larry Bird, Julius Erving, and other superstars. In fact, I hit the game-winning shot, driving past Larry Bird and banking a jumper over the outstretched arm of Magic Johnson.

Five . . .
Four . . .
Three . . .
Two . . .
One . . .
(Swish)
Buzzerrrrrrrrrrrrrrrrrrr.

Talk about living the dream—and it had nothing to do with REM sleep either. This really happened. I honestly played against Larry Bird and Magic Johnson. I promise. It wasn't a celebrity charity game for over-the-hill adults either. I played against them when they were in their prime—and I was only seventeen.

Actually, I played against those superstars every day. Those were the names I gave the different pine trees around my backyard basketball court, the one that was all dirt because I killed the grass by playing so much. Tree Rollins played for the Atlanta Hawks at the time, so he was a perfect fit. You wouldn't believe how many times I abused Bird and Johnson. Their bark was always worse than their bite.

Pine trees named Larry Bird and Magic Johnson are partly responsible for this book. Looking back, I realize now how silly it was that a kid almost out of high school was still living in Nylon Narnia, a fantasyland that sheltered me from having to think about what was coming next in the real world. My only goal was a basketball goal.

Maybe you're there, in your own private cover-up. Maybe you're unsure of what's next and are scared to think about it. I understand, and I'd like to offer some encouragement.

~

When I was stuck in life-limbo, basketball was my outlet to avoid dealing with real issues like schoolwork, tests, and planning for college and a career. I learned the importance of decision making the hard way. I learned that nondecision—refusal to responsibly think and act—is really a decision. I chose to idly sit back and let life happen. Before long, life began leaving me behind.

The first letter in our acrostic of D-R-E-A-M stands for *Decisions*. Life is a series of decisions—some inconsequential, some life altering. Your decisions will shape who you are, as I began discovering before I left high school.

I don't know why I was attracted to basketball or how it caught my attention. I wasn't super tall. I wasn't fast. And I wasn't particularly good, though I did become the starting point guard at North Clayton High School outside of Atlanta. My whole life became wrapped up in this sport dominated by big men and fast, skillful athletes. All of my high school dreams focused on basketball. I wasn't as good as I probably thought I was, and the talent level required to play in college was too great. In basketball, the shorter the player, the lower the ceiling.

In my mind and in my heart I was the next Pete Maravich. I would spend hours in the backyard by myself, dodging the defensive efforts of the thin pine (Julius Erving), the thick pine (Larry Bird), and the extra-thick pine (Magic Johnson). I'd drive by one of them and shoot a jumper and make it to win the game every time. And when I missed, there was always a late foul or just enough time to rebound and call a time-out.

Too bad life doesn't work that way, as I would soon learn.

When I neared graduation and basketball remained the only focal point of my life, it was a shock when those hoop dreams collapsed. I realized that basketball wasn't going to get me an education even at a small college. Making matters worse, I had been so consumed with basketball that I had skated by in school. I passed, but that was about it. I cared little about homework or tests, and my SAT score reflected my disinterest. I did just enough to get by.

That's when it hit me.

Well, what am I going to do with the rest of my life? What am I going to be?

I was so jarred that my questions led to other questions, which in my soul-searching eventually led to the biggest question: *Why did God put me here? I need to find out.*

Suddenly I looked through the window into my backyard and couldn't see Larry Bird and Magic Johnson for the trees. They were tall and thick and made a mess with their pine needles all over my pristine basketball court, all over my fantasies. It seemed like a different kind of clock was counting down, one that was full of real pressure. . . .

Five . . .

Four . . .

Three . . .

Two . . .

Would I make it?

I was yet to learn what it means to live the true dream. But the searching had begun—a process that would take me from the dirt court in my backyard to pastoring a church with more than four thousand members and overseeing an academy of more than thirteen hundred students. In between came the decisions. Millions of life-shaping decisions.

I'd like to help you with decision making. In fact, in the next chapter are two very important principles I want you to remember every single time you are mulling over something. Why?

Because Decision Time is always 5:15.

What Time Is It?

I was almost a bean counter. I could pass for one now. I most certainly didn't look like one then.

I wound up at Georgia Southern College (now a university) originally because I left so few options available to me that I had to default to what my dad did for a living. I went to school to become an accountant.

Yeah, I know. I yawned too.

But I couldn't think of anything else. Actually, I could think of something else . . . but I didn't want to listen to the still small voice whispering in my ear, constantly, incessantly drawing me ever since the night I walked up my stairway after listening to Billy Graham on TV. Ultimately, one crucial decision led me to Mercer University, where I majored in religious studies. My time at Georgia Southern was beneficial, however, because I received an eye-opening tutorial in decision making. The Lord let me learn not only from my many mistakes, but also from the terrible decisions of others.

I grew up in church. My parents trudged me through the doors every time they were open, for which I am now grateful. I possessed a solid biblical foundation by the time I reached college and encountered all that campus life entails. That was a good thing.

I needed every ounce of conviction and wisdom I had ever received to steer clear of the traps that consumed so many others.

Despite moving to a new city while in high school, I still enjoyed a comfort zone and a certain identity constructed around family, home, sports, classes, and, eventually, a few new friends. When I arrived at Georgia Southern, I had to start from scratch. I knew no one. My roommate was a guy I had hung around with for about six months during the tenth grade. I barely knew him, but suddenly I was living with him. Everyone else was a complete stranger.

While I was not an intellectual, I was what many in Georgia would call "a good boy." God was working in my life, slowly impressing His direction for me. That, combined with a lifetime of biblical education in church, meant my decision making stood out from the crowd.

I was called "Preacher." Most fraternities asked me to join so they would have a religious guy during public ceremonies. Everyone seemed committed to see how many parties they could attend and how much liberty they could express. For the first time in their lives, they weren't tethered to a leash, and their claims to freedom oozed from their pores.

Meanwhile, back at the dorm . . .

I was the guy everyone called to come pick them up at the bar or frat party and drive them home.

More than ever, as I struggled to come to terms with the Lord's ever-growing work in my life, I realized that the biggest question facing me—facing all of the students around me—was not "What am I going to do with my life?" No, the more important question trumped any talk of majors or careers or fraternity affiliations or party plans. It wouldn't go away. Some people ignored it, but with increasing force it shouted me down. . . .

WHO am I going to be?

I observed that most other students had majors, but that emphasis really wasn't the priority of their lives. Instead, consciously or subconsciously, they focused on behavior. They spent time deciding whether they were going to be a party guy or a serious student. They were choosing habits—work habits, study habits, sleep habits, eating habits—that would impact them for the next five or six decades. At the time, they didn't think those decisions were critical. Now that they're forty-five years old, they would tell a different story.

They may not have realized it then, but they were struggling with the same question: "Who am I going to be? Now that I'm in this atmosphere and making decisions on my own—probably more than I want to make—and I have all of this peer pressure, who am I going to be?"

That's why I've come to the conclusion that Decision Time is always 5:15. Not 5:15 AM to start your morning or 5:15 PM at the end of the day. Decision Time is 5:15 because we are wise to run every decision through the filter of two important principles found in 2 Corinthians 5:15 and Ephesians 5:15.

And he died for all, that those who live should no longer live for themselves but for him who died for them and was raised again. (2 Corinthians 5:15)

Be very careful, then, how you live—not as unwise but as wise. (Ephesians 5:15)

Memorize these verses. Then, to help you remember to use them when struggling with a decision, get in the habit of asking yourself, "What time is it?"

It's 5:15.

There is one decision you must make that supersedes all other decisions. It will determine whether any other decision you ever make is successful.

The only authentic way to decide who you are is first to decide who Jesus Christ is. Not everyone believes it, but the entire universe hinges upon His identity.

You have to do something with Him. You either must agree with who He says He is and submit to Him, or refute who He says He is and deny His lordship in your life. You can't just ignore Him, thinking you'll address it later. Remember, indecision is a decision. Ignoring Christ means saying, "No, thank you."

I'm reminded of a stirring passage written by C. S. Lewis, the brilliant twentieth-century Irish philosopher who finally accepted the claims of Christ after years of searching and listening to the witness of friend J. R. R. Tolkien of *Lord of the Rings* fame.

> I am trying here to prevent anyone saying the really foolish thing that people often say about Him: "I'm ready to accept Jesus as a great moral teacher, but I don't accept His claim to be God." That is one thing we must not say. A man who was merely a man and said the sort of things Jesus said would not be a great moral teacher. He would either be a lunatic—on a level with the man who says he is a poached egg—or else he would be the Devil of Hell. You must make your choice. Either this man was, and is, the Son of God; or else a madman or something worse. You can shut Him up for a fool, you can spit at Him and kill Him as a demon; or you can fall at His feet and call Him Lord and God. But let us not come with any patronizing nonsense about His being a great human teacher. He has not left that open to us. He did not intend to.[1]

The person who has accepted Christ's claims and surrendered to Him must, by reborn nature, honor 2 Corinthians 5:15. He died for us. That means, out of sheer devotion in gratitude, we should no longer live for ourselves. Rather, we should give our lives, our every decision, to the One who first gave His life to us.

Next, Ephesians 5:15 reminds us to be careful and wise.

If you are a believer, do you fly by the seat of your pants—or do you carefully weigh decisions? I'm not referring to wringing your hands over trifling matters. I'm referring to faithfully spending time in prayer and Bible study, seeking God's counsel and wisdom.

I've heard people complain, "I want to grow deeper in my walk, but all I ever hear preachers say is pray and read the Bible."

Right.

I've learned that God speaks most often through three ways: His Word, His Holy Spirit, and circumstances. The best way to hear from God is through His Word. The best way for Him to hear from you is through prayer.

Do you make sure to "be very careful" how you live?

Being careful means habitually spending time in God's Word and prayer. Being careful means waiting on the Lord to make the picture clear. It means diligently examining circumstances and squaring them with Scripture. Being careful means seeking the counsel of godly friends and adults (but please make sure they're godly, and if anyone ever gives you counsel that goes against Scripture, ignore it—it's not from God).

You may say, "I've turned to the Bible to help me with a decision, but I couldn't find anything that fit my situation." I've heard that one before. That's why effective Bible study is habitual Bible study. Over time, its deep truths, which apply to every situation, will sink in. It won't change your circumstances, but it will change you.

For example, you may face the dilemma of whether to accompany friends to a party at Darrell's lake house. The Bible doesn't say, "Don't go to Darrell's party."

But it does tell you to avoid even the appearance of evil (1 Thessalonians 5:22 KJV).

It does remind you to hate evil and cling to good (Romans 12:9).

It does remind you that your body is the temple of the Holy Spirit, who dwells within you, and that you are not your own (1 Corinthians 6:19).

Would the Holy Spirit be comfortable at that party? You need to answer that honestly, because you'll carry Him there.

The Bible offers clear principles to demonstrate the wisdom of avoiding such scenes. The Bible renews your mind (Romans 12:2) and steers your decision making. This is why regular Bible study is essential. The Holy Spirit will use God's Word to prompt you at just the right time, every time. He will help you stop and think, *Because of who I am and whom I serve, I choose to make this decision.*

Operating within this framework helps determine who you are going to be. Then you can entertain questions like, "What am I going to do for a living?" These questions bear less gravity. They're not *un*important. They're just not *as* important. They don't define you. When someone asks, "Who are you?" you should not respond by saying, "Well, I'm a student" or "I'm a technician," or "I'm a stay-at-home mom." That's what you do, but it's not your identity.

Your identity is forged by clawing down to the foundational decision of whom you serve—God or self—and what kind of person you're going to be. Ask yourself, "Am I going to live for myself or am I going to live for God? Am I going to be wholly devoted to Jesus or am I going to fit into the crowd? Am I going to be a leader or a follower?"

The answers to those kinds of questions not only shape your decision making but also pave the only path toward living the dream God has in store for you.

But beware . . . there is one kind of decision that is a dream destroyer.

If you choose to live a self-serving life, then you're going to miss the dream. I don't care how "good" life may seem; you'll still fall short of the dream God has for you.

You can be the CEO of the company, the star of the show, or the all-American athlete and still be outside of God's will and, therefore, unfulfilled. Everyone has heard the stories of men and women who have climbed the ladder and made it to the heights of success only to look back down at everyone and proclaim, "It's empty. It's not what I thought it was going to be."

The reason is because they're living the *American* dream. People admire their lives and envy them. But they've missed *the* dream—God's dream—because they've missed God's design for them. Unfortunately, too many people acknowledge the emptiness of it all only when they're gasping for their last breaths.

At some point, you indeed must answer the question, "What am I going to do?" But before facing that decision, you must answer more pressing questions: "Who am I going to be? Am I going to be someone who follows my own drumbeat? Or am I going to pursue God's heartbeat? Am I going to seek to discover God's desire for me and then commit to follow the path He has carved for me?"

Or are you going to hit a little Fleetwood Mac on the iPod and "Go Your Own Way"?

Once you choose to honor God by living out His dream, then the answer to the question of what you will do begins to take shape. In fact, it often becomes instantly apparent.

The big decision, the identity decision, already has been made. Everything else pales in comparison. Whatever you do is only a part of your life. But who you're going to be is *all* of your life. It's who you are.

Most people get it backward. They let what they *do* define who they're going to *be*. The proper response is to pursue God's dream for you—to decide who you're going to be—and let it define how you go about what you do. The proper response is one simple question: What time is it?

Now, are you ready for a challenge?

DREAM Challenge:

God gave you the right to choose . . . so take it!

One of my favorite scenes in the movie *Spider-Man* is when Peter Parker's uncle Ben is driving him downtown and they have a disagreement. I didn't appreciate how Peter disrespected his loving uncle, but I did appreciate the wisdom and restraint of the senior man in the face of a young man bursting at the seams to assert his independence.

By this point in the movie, Peter already knows he has special powers endued by a radioactive spider's bite. Uncle Ben doesn't know about Peter's supernatural abilities, yet he makes a comment that resonates with Peter for the remainder of the movie: "With great power comes great responsibility."

As you enter full-blown adulthood, you harbor great power.

This power comes with the independence you have craved. You have the power to change things—to change the world. You have the power to improve it or harm it. You have the power to help others or hurt them. You have the power to be an investor or a spender. You have the power to be a filler or a drainer.

You have the power to decide.

There is an old quote by an unknown person that says, "The whole world steps aside for the man who knows where he is going."

You have the power to make the whole world step aside.

Do you know where you're going?

Actually, you have a choice to make before you begin making choices. You have the option of living for the Lord or living for yourself. You have the option of operating in submission to God and His Word—or ignoring Him and plowing ahead on your own. And don't be fooled . . . He will allow you to go it alone. He knows that it is for your best, because when (not if) you hit enough walls, you more likely will turn to Him.

God made us in His image. That means He gave us intellect, reason, emotions, and a will to choose (or else we would be robots; what love is there in that?). You can choose the will of the Savior, or you can crown yourself king and choose the will of self.

We hear much about the *right* to choose these days—and we do have the right of choice. We just need to remember who gave us the right. God did. Not Thomas Jefferson or other founding forefathers.

God.

So you must exercise your right. You must choose: Will you flourish or flounder? The psalmist explains in Psalm 1 that we are not to walk with the wicked or with sinners or mockers. Instead, if the believer will delight in God's Word, He promises him a *lifetime* of blessings, a lifetime of living the dream:

He is like a tree planted by streams of water, which yields its fruit in season and whose leaf does not wither. Whatever he does prospers. (Psalm 1:3)

Proverbs 4:25–26 reminds us to keep our eyes focused on the dream.

It tells us to let our eyes gaze directly ahead rather than be distracted with all of the world's charms. It encourages us to walk the firm and level path even though it is much narrower than the wider, easier path. That path is full of hidden peril. That path appears to have solid ground, but Satan has strategically customized sinkholes and quicksand at just the perfect locales to fit your personality and weaknesses (and sometimes your strengths). He is the master manipulator, the ultimate deceiver who comes to steal, kill, and destroy—and the sad news is that he targets young people because he knows that if he can wreck them early, he can impact their entire lives.

I know of a young lady who attended the University of Georgia. When she arrived on campus as a freshman, she had more freedom than ever before. She was no longer under the daily supervision of her parents. She took it as an opportunity to dive into sin. She ended up in jail and expelled from school. Sometime later, after she tasted the salt of her tears and felt the dankness of a cell floor, she made another critical decision.

She chose God's path to reordering her life. Now the same university asks her to return and speak to students about the pitfalls of the road most traveled.

God's grace is sufficient, and He does forgive sin. But He also has instituted a universal law that cannot be violated: "Do not be deceived, God is not mocked; for whatever a man sows, that he will also reap" (Galatians 6:7 NKJV). There are consequences to sin, and sin is a decision. For example, premarital sex can be forgiven, but there remains a spiritual union in sex that requires giving oneself away, and that can never be regained. It also will mean carrying forward into the marriage bed the impact and baggage of every previous act.

The same young lady who stumbled at the University of Georgia will tell you that our God is a redeeming, loving God (which is why He let her come to the end of herself). Yet she also would say she could have saved herself a lot of heartache by following Him sooner.

The writer of Psalm 119 anticipated our next question.

How can a young man keep his way pure? By living according to your word. (Psalm 119:9)

I've been asked how I approach decision making. First, I try to keep the process simple.

I ask, "What does the Bible say about this area of my life? Is there a guiding principle that I need to think about before I act?"

Next, because making decisions can be stressful, I try to invoke the 5:15 Decision Time principles outlined in the previous chapter while also following the pattern of Philippians 4:6–8. In one sentence, the apostle Paul instructs us to pray, make petitions, and present our requests. Sounds like he's serious about this prayer business. God wants us to be narrow-minded in decision making. He wants us to narrow our focus onto Him alone.

The key to the passage is a two-word phrase—"with thanksgiving."

A proper attitude in prayer is to thank God for His answer ahead of time—whatever His will. Whether it's in line with my idea or against my idea, I should thank Him for His response because I'm grateful for His guidance and can trust that a loving God has my best at heart. My thanksgiving also is an explicit agreement that I plan to follow His leadership.

How can we not follow such a great God, one who gives us all things—even the right to choose?

The Philippians passage is highlighted by one of the most claimed promises in all of Scripture. "And the peace of God, which transcends all understanding, will guard your hearts and your minds in Christ Jesus" (v. 7).

The peace of God is indescribable and will come without fail when we make godly decisions.

Sometimes God allows the pressure to remain until we follow His certain direction, but sometimes either choice is within His will. Sometimes when we're torn, the friction isn't coming from Him but from the enemy, who wants to keep us agitated, unmoved, and ineffective for God's kingdom.

However, the God of all peace will lavish His peace on the petitioner who is pursuing His will, following His Word, and living His way.

That peace often signals our answer. At other times, it clears the way for us to choose among multiple solutions within God's will. Whatever the case, a peace that transcends understanding is one that is mind-boggling. Suddenly, we stop striving and trying to fix everything ourselves and wedging all the pieces into a less-than-perfect fit.

We take a deep breath and realize that *God gave us the right to choose*. As long as our choices reflect the One who granted us the gift of choice, we can be assured that He is with us.

Fear slinks away. Sleep descends easier. The day dawns brighter. And living the dream becomes a more vibrant reality than ever.

DREAM Resolution:

I will exercise my God-given right to choose by:

_____

_____

_____

_____

_____

_____

I will memorize the following Scripture to help me make decisions:

_____

_____

_____

_____

_____

_____

relationships

Drunks don't keep curfew.

I realized this only after landing on my head in the floorboard of my blue 1970 AMC Javelin. A drunk driver had plowed into the rear of my precious first car shortly after midnight on a Saturday during my junior year of high school. It was 1978. I had new vinyl seat covers and a paint job so dead that every time I washed my car the water in the bucket turned blue. Sort of like my forehead after it hit the floorboard.

I lay there stunned, peering at the dome light above. In an instant, my world literally was turned upside down. The view from the bottom of teenage rebellion can be ugly.

I remember the smell of gas. It ran out of my punctured tank onto the asphalt of Highway 138 in the growing Georgia hamlet of Riverdale.

I remember I had been waiting for an oncoming car to pass so I could turn left into the subdivision of my friend Jeff Mitchum, whom I was taking home.

I remember checking my rearview mirror seconds earlier and seeing nothing.

I remember that there were no screeching tires, no warning signs.

I remember the eerie silence after the instanta-neous and thunderous crash.

I remember the shuffle of a drunk and the slur of his speech as he checked on his victims.

And I remember the anxiety of realizing, even before the crash, that I was already in trouble.

Disobedient teens don't keep curfew either.

I was in a crash because I was out past the curfew my parents had set for me. I was out past curfew because I had made one, just one, bad decision. I made a bad decision because I so hungered for friendship.

I arrived on top of my head on my floorboard through a series of events that began months earlier. My father's job in accounting transferred from Tal-lahassee to Atlanta in the summer before my tenth-grade year. We moved first to Clarkston, on the east side of Atlanta, but lived in an apartment while my parents shopped for a home. I made a few acquain-tances but no real friends my entire sophomore year. I knew not to put down any roots; the apartment in Clarkston was a mere way station.

Instead, I retreated to basketball. It became my only friend.

Through my first fifteen years, friendship was inherent. I didn't have to work at it. I grew up in a Tallahassee neighborhood with nine boys, all of similar age, all full of life. We played together, rode bikes together, went to school together, went to the movies together, did everything together. My relationships were on cruise control until Dad's job moved us.

Suddenly I was in Clarkston and alone. It took months just to make a few buddies. Those connections were welcome, though superficial. With only three weeks remaining in the school year, and just when I was beginning to make a little progress, my parents finally found a home—on the other side of Atlanta.

Over those final three weeks of tenth grade at North Clayton High School in Riverdale, I made a few acquaintances, but basically I got up every day, went to school, ate lunch quietly, came home, and headed to a basketball hoop at a local park. When my junior year started, I still didn't know anyone. I realized that I was going to have to *choose* some friends. That's what all teenagers and adults must do—choose relationships.

I started reaching out. Just as it was natural to make friends in my neighborhood when I was a boy, I resorted to my familiar surroundings and began cultivating relationships with other guys on the basketball team.

And then it happened.

Still in a vulnerable stage, I let down my guard after an out-of-town basketball game. When we returned to our school, we had unloaded our bus when one of the guys said, "Hey, John is having a party at his house. Let's all go over there." My curfew time of 11 PM wasn't unreasonable, even on a Friday with an away game. I remember thinking, *I know I have a curfew, but I've got to make some friends. I'll just blow curfew and go with these guys. I'll explain myself to Dad later.*

Before I knew it, out came the words: "Hey, I'll drive."

I drove my Javelin with the dead blue paint to John's house. Curfew came. I knew it because I kept glancing at my watch. The reason I was monitoring my watch is because I knew my dad waited up for me at home. But I was willing to bear the consequences just to make a few friends.

My newfound courage lasted all of half an hour. I was so sweating the blown curfew that I finally corralled my basketball buddies and said, "Guys, I've got to take y'all home." They wanted to stay. All except for Jeff Mitchum said they would find a ride home.

Jeff and I climbed into the Javelin and headed toward his home. We were four houses away from Jeff's place when the drunk provided proof—90 proof—that my dad had been right all those years: "Nothing good happens after midnight."

The drunk was going sixty miles per hour. My car, which had been at a complete stop, wound up several yards down the highway. Jeff and I weren't wearing seat belts—we were invincible, see—and we landed headfirst on the floorboard.

The drunk staggered to my car and asked if we were all right before he fled the scene. Jeff and I walked to his home and phoned the police. Then I called my dad. He answered immediately.

"Hey, Dad. This is Tim."

"Tim who?"

"What do you mean, who? Your son, Tim."

"Hmm. Nope. Not my son, Tim."

"What do you mean? I'm calling you from Jeff Mitchum's house."

"No, my son came home an hour ago. He's probably in bed asleep because he's got a curfew."

I sighed.

"Okay, Dad. I didn't keep curfew. I stayed out too late. And now I've wrecked the car."

He paused.

"Is anybody hurt?" he asked.

"No."

"Where are you?"

I told him.

"I'll be there in a minute."

I hung up the phone and stood there, stewing—not at Dad but at myself. *For the first time in my life I'd had to choose friends, and I made the wrong choice.*

I had let fear force me into making bad choices for relationships. They weren't the worst guys, but I was willing to do anything just to have friends, just to be accepted. That's when I began to realize that relationships can be dangerous. We may think that we're only making friends for a season, but relationships can impact us for a lifetime.

It was right about the time that I was peeling myself off my floorboard amid a sea of glass shards that an ancient Hebrew proverb rang true:

He who walks with the wise grows wise, but a companion of fools suffers harm. (Proverbs 13:20)

What did I learn from my travelin' Javelin escapade? I slowly began to learn (too slowly) to tread more deliberately through the furrows of friendship. It doesn't take long for roots to grow, whether on good, dressed soil or in the briar patch. I began to learn something I still try to put into practice: Choose friends wisely because they become your in-crowd.

Allow me to introduce you to the in-crowd. . . .

Giving Yourself Away

It can seem so vital in high school—and beyond—to be a part of the in-crowd. Almost everyone judges you based on whom you associate with.

If you run with the jocks, you're considered a jock, regardless of whether you're athletic. Some of those guys and girls are wannabes, but they're still "jocks."

Are you a cheerleader? Then you're considered a chosen one, fairer than most to the mirror on the wall.

If you hang with the computer geeks, you're considered to have a lifetime membership in the *Dungeons and Dragons* club.

If you drive around with the stoners, everyone assumes that cloud of smoke didn't come from the muffler.

Even if the designations morph somewhat as we mature, the principle still applies: We are who our friends are. We go to the same places and do the same things. It's human nature. I just happen to think that we view this aspect of human nature from an inverted perspective.

Most people look at cliques and consider what they can get out of the club. *What's in it for me?* A more illuminating view is to consider what the club will get out of us. What will it *require* of us?

Being part of the in-crowd doesn't require staking out your territory and claiming your identity turf nearly as much as it requires you to give yourself away. It reminds me of the bridge in the U2 song "With or Without You."

> **And you give yourself away . . .**
> **And you give . . .**
> **And you give . . .**
> **And you give yourself away . . .**

The Christian group Third Day has sampled that lyric in concert before, but they've done it in reference to Jesus. The original song recalls only a wistful relationship in which the singer laments, "I can't live . . . with or without you." Too often we base our identities on what we do and the people with whom we associate, as if we truly cannot live without them. Adults are every bit as guilty as high school sophomores—because you don't grow out of human nature after high school.

We must remember that we live and move and *have our being* in God. Because of this truth, friendship assumes even greater weight; we've already yielded to the Holy Spirit, so we must carefully consider whom else we'll allow inside our hearts.

Participation with the in-crowd has at least four levels in which we increasingly give ourselves away. All begin with the prefix "in."

Involvement

Friendship begins with involvement, and involvement sometimes doesn't observe the speed limit.

We often do not realize the depths to which we have allowed other people's lives to intertwine with ours. We don't grasp how the significance of a singular relationship can escalate. In making a friend, we gradually give him permission to impact us on some level with his wisdom—or lack thereof—and his rationale, judgment, intellect, ideas, and morals—or lack thereof.

I learned this in a near life-altering way when involvement suddenly gave way to the next stage. . . .

Influence

The amount of influence your friends own in your life depends on one element.

You.

Influence becomes power when it is yielded: "Aw, c'mon, man. Let's do this. . . . Let's go here or there. . . . It's not going to hurt just to try this."

Long before he died in 2005, the great Memphis preacher Adrian Rogers drawled that a person's influence is so powerful it bears eternal consequence: "If you go to heaven, you'll most likely take someone with you through your influence. But if you go to hell, you'll most likely take someone to hell with you."[1]

Then Dr. Rogers quoted Romans 14:7: "For none of us lives to himself alone and none of us dies to himself alone."

Most often, influence is referred to as peer pressure. It can be so prevalent that we don't need a relationship with someone to feel its force. We want to do what "everyone else" is doing. Yet when the pressure comes from someone with whom we are developing a friendship, the pressure increases dramatically.

That's why I came close to getting burned one night.

My job at McDonald's brought more paycheck than pride, but I did it because the company's hours were flexible and I could both play basketball and work. Because of practices and games, I was placed on the crew that closed the store at night. One of those evenings stands out in my memory because of a few co-workers with whom I had become involved. Once again, I made friends in a certain setting only because it was convenient. Bad idea. It just came naturally for me because that's what happened in my boyhood—the guys in my neighborhood became my friends. The guys I worked with? They became my friends.

As time passed with the McDonald's crew, we began hanging out in the parking lot after closing the restaurant at 2 AM. One of my new buddies, Bobby, drove a Volkswagen Beetle. I had known Bobby a little bit because we attended the same church.

On this night, we sat in his car listening to music. I was there for one reason: I wanted to be cool and hang out like everyone else. We sat in our cars, rolled down our windows, played music, and chatted between cars. Seems innocent enough, right?

I would soon discover that allowing someone's involvement in your life can also mean allowing *their* involvement with other people. This is why influence is one willing heartbeat away from . . .

Intimacy

Mere involvement can have ripples on your life. Intimacy can create Richter-scale tremors.

The American Heritage Dictionary states that intimacy is "marked by close acquaintance or familiarity," and goes on to assert that it means something or someone is "essential" and "innermost."

So in this third stage we not only have reached the in-crowd but also the innermost crowd. This is a more crucial level because intimacy requires offering and demanding a degree of trust as we yield ourselves even more. We are more willing to believe at face value, we are more willing to surrender ourselves, we are more willing to sacrifice—in short, we are more willing to accept. At this stage, friends begin to reveal the inside scoop on their character. They begin to take off some of the makeup from their warts.

I came dangerously close to intimacy that night in the McDonald's parking lot.

As we sat in Bobby's Beetle, someone else drove up, someone who knew my new buddies. He began passing out marijuana cigarettes. I refused when he offered one to me. One reason I didn't take a toke was because I could envision it being one of those nights when my dad met me at the front door, regardless of the hour. There was no way the pungency of pot would get past him. So when they all lit up, I got out of Bobby's car and climbed into my car, a 1972 Chevelle that had replaced the wrecked Javelin.

At this point, there were three cars parked side-by-side. I was alone in my car. I was still in the group and trying to cling to something that resembled coolness, but inside I was scared. I watched as they all passed the dope. I was uncomfortable, but not uncomfortable enough to stop compromising. I wanted friends. I wanted to be accepted.

Out of the corner of my eye, I saw in my rearview mirror the headlights of a slow-moving vehicle pulling up behind my car. When I saw it turn, I realized immediately who it was. It was Bobby's dad . . .

The pastor of our church.

Bobby's dad was also the chaplain of the police department, and a patrol car was tailing him. I didn't stick around to watch this family affair. As soon as I recognized the pastor's car, I cranked my Chevelle and took off toward home. I realize now that this probably made me look guilty; it's just as well, because I already *felt* guilty and had not responded to that God-given warning signal.

I had been one second, one lapse, from extending my arm and taking hold of an illegal drug. I was one second from intimacy, from knowing and being known, just as Eve was when she indeed extended her arm and took hold of that which was forbidden (Genesis 3:1–6).

When I reached home, I ignored the clock and walked into my parents' bedroom.

"Let me tell you what just happened," I said as they squinted at me, their parent-hearts racing through that breathless moment of wondering exactly what was about to come out of their child's mouth.

"I don't know if they're going to knock on our door in a minute or not, but we were hanging out in the McDonald's parking lot, and . . . "

And . . . I know, I know. Nothing good happens after midnight.

Investment

Intimacy easily spirals into investment, which verifies that relationships bear immeasurable impact on who God wants you to be and why those choices are vital.

Here's why: Friends with whom you share some measure of intimacy will make an investment in who you are. They will pour into your life something, whether good or bad, from the reservoir of their souls. They, like you, are giving part of themselves away, and at this stage each of you is willing to receive what the other offers.

We all have seen the subtle evidence: Hannah begins hanging out with Jenny. They share maybe one or two common interests but aren't all that similar at first. Before long, they're emphasizing those common interests, and those interests begin shaping their whole character. Gradually, imperceptibly, Hannah starts using words that Jenny uses. Jenny begins dressing like Hannah. They begin sharing common habits, mannerisms, and quirks. Even their speech patterns—their accents and stress on certain syllables—mimic the other's talk. Their tone of voice becomes almost identical. People rarely mention one without the other.

People rarely mention one without the other.
Who is your in-crowd?

Do people rarely mention you without another? Do they rarely mention the other without mentioning you?

Are you comfortable with that? Are you sure?

First Corinthians 15:33 offers an important reminder: "Do not be misled: 'Bad company corrupts good character.' "

On the night I could've become a McPothead, I stood in my parents' bedroom and realized yet again that friendship is the stuff of which lifetimes are made. If it's the right friend, it's beautiful. If it's the wrong one, it's ruinous. I didn't participate in anything illegal. I didn't do what they did, and I didn't really want to do it. But I was there. I was sitting right there. And I was a breath away from trying drugs, investing in the lives of people I hardly knew—and allowing a complete stranger to invest in mine—and possibly having a criminal record.

My world had changed when my family moved from Tallahassee, and as a stranger in a strange place I gambled because my teenage heart so yearned to be accepted.

The greatest tragedy was that I didn't realize I already was.

DREAM Challenge:

Extend your hands but protect your heart.

This section's challenge is at once freeing and frank:

Open your life to new friends. Have fun. Go for it. There are few rewards greater than those forged in friendships.

Just protect your heart at the same time.

Be smart. Guard your heart and mind with God's Word and the wisdom gleaned from it. Slather your life in prayer. Let the Holy Spirit make your friends for you.

I'm not saying be super spiritual. Don't be aloof. Don't be a prude.

Be real.

And being real means allowing the living, loving God of the universe to live out His life through you at all times and in every way—in every relationship. If you're saved, you have all of God in you that you're going to get. The Holy Spirit isn't on a dividend plan. He doesn't come piecemeal. You either have all of Him or you have none of Him.

The question is: How much of *you* does the Holy Spirit have? How much of your life, including your relationships, are you willing to surrender?

You may have to die to some habits, preferences, or inclinations. You may have to get out of what has been your comfort zone.

You just may have to let go . . . of everything.

Isn't that freeing?

Exciting?

Challenging?

Isn't that the only life worth living?

Proverbs 4:23 supports the DREAM Challenge:

Above all else, guard your heart, for it is the wellspring of life.

Out of your heart spring all of the issues of your life, including relationships. Out of your heart spring choices and habits. The condition of your heart, then, determines the quality of your relationships, choices, and habits. It determines the quality and impact of your life.

Samuel Johnston was one of our nation's Christian forefathers. He was the governor of North Carolina from 1787 to 1789 and a member of the Continental Congress in 1780–81. He never uttered more profound words in office or debate than when he said, "True happiness consists not in a multitude of friends, but in their worth and choice."

It's up to you. What will be the worth and choice of your friends?

I have had to choose new friends on several occasions. One of those was in my first year at Georgia Southern College in Statesboro, Georgia.

For the first time, I was on my own, living away from home and my parents, and having to fend for myself. Looking back, I realize how vulnerable I was, and I understand better how God's grace sustained me for my one year in Statesboro.

I remember the almost electric atmosphere of that time. The feeling of independence was thrilling—though mixed with more than a tinge of apprehension at what tomorrow may bring. It was important that I anchor myself in solid friendships.

Everyone in my dorm, classes, and cafeteria was a complete stranger, which was exciting in a way. I now realize it also was dangerous, because alliances come easy when you're homesick and suffering loneliness for the first time. I got passing grades in choosing some of my friends; I'm sad to say that others were of the remedial variety.

I would like to share a few truths that, had I known then, would've helped me adjust.

Throughout the difficult transition days of high school and college, when I often found myself staring at new faces in new territory, my heart's foremost yearning was to be accepted. I craved in-crowd status and made a few compromises as a result. Only later, as my fellowship with Christ strengthened, did I discover that my best Friend had already accepted me.

I knew I was saved and going to heaven after I surrendered my heart to Jesus at age eleven. I just didn't grasp that I was actually accepted by a Friend who sticks closer than a brother. The first chapter of Ephesians explains this illuminating truth:

Blessed be the God and Father of our Lord Jesus Christ, who has blessed us with every spiritual blessing in the heavenly places in Christ, just as He chose us in Him before the foundation of the world, that we should be holy and without blame before Him in love, having predestined us to adoption as sons by Jesus Christ to Himself, according to the good pleasure of His will, to the praise of the glory of His grace, by which He made us accepted in the Beloved. (Ephesians 1:3–6 NKJV)

If you are a believer, God chose you before He created the world. It's a mind-boggling thought, but He already had decided He would adopt you as a son or daughter.

Until I was an adult, I didn't comprehend this truth. I didn't realize I was accepted in the Beloved and didn't need to derive my identity from anything or anyone else. Notice the capital "B" in the word

Beloved. That's another name for Jesus. Jesus accepts me, no matter what.

That removes the pressure. I can rely on Him in what should be my *priority relationship*. When that cornerstone is in place, life and its many varied pieces and persons fall together in ways that are much more fluid and less forced.

Much more friendly. Much more fun.

Speaking of fun, our next section carries us to the source of the stuff.

DREAM Resolution:

I will extend my hands toward others but protect my heart in these ways:

_____

_____

_____

_____

_____

_____

enthusiasm

Part of the mystery behind the struggle to find my way in life was that I had never been allergic to gusto. I had never been lackadaisical or even lazy. I had rarely sported a careless attitude.

I was gridlocked not because of a lack of effort, but because of a lack of effort in the right pursuits. I was bewildered as I stood at the crossroads of young adulthood, and I shuddered at the potential outcomes. One major ingredient helped bring me out of my funk.

Enthusiasm.

I benefited from an undercurrent of zeal for life and a hunger to succeed. I suspect that you have that same longing for a full life, that same taste for God's best. It may seem buried deep below, but it's there.

Growing up I enjoyed healthy injections of the proper attitude toward effort and determination. My father was always ready with words that were supportive, instructive, or corrective, depending upon the situation. . . .

Pay attention.

Give it your all.

Wherever you are, be all there.

Then we moved from Florida to Atlanta, and I started my sophomore year as a nobody in a hallway of somebodies. Everyone seemed to know everyone else—but me. I retreated to what I did know, basketball, and learned a few life lessons along the way. One of them was proof that my dad knew what he was talking about.

~

The first time I came face-to-face with him was just a week or two after I moved to Atlanta. He was tall, probably six feet four. He carried himself like he personally had laid the brick and mortar of the gymnasium, and when he spoke—when he boomed— everyone else grew quiet. Even the basketballs stopped dribbling as his voice echoed off the steel rafters. His athletic build only intensified his aura.

His name was Coach Larabus. I still don't know his full name. The first item on the sports agenda when I started my new school at Clarkston High was the introductory meeting between the coaches and the kids interested in playing their respective sports.

I went to Coach Larabus's basketball meeting. He was an intimidating, Bobby Knight kind of guy. Bobby Knight is known for throwing a chair across the court. Coach Larabus is known for staring a hole through a chair. I didn't mind. I sat there and thought, *Drive me hard, that's fine by me. Make me mad, I'll just play harder.* When he watched me at tryouts, he decided I was a keeper. I'll never forget his words: "Well, you have some talent and maybe you can help us. I'm going to work with you."

I soon earned a spot as a starter on the junior varsity team. I remember how scared I was when I walked onto the court for our first game. After tip-off, it showed. I was horrible, and I wondered if Coach Larabus would reconsider his decision not to cut me. Instead, he approached me afterward with a surprising offer.

"Hey, if you can come in before school, I'm going to work with you and turn this around," he said. "You just need to get over your fear."

He began tutoring me in the mornings. Before school started, we'd do all kinds of shooting and ball-handling drills. Because of his individual attention, I turned a lot of corners. By the tenth game of the season I had improved so much that he promoted me to varsity. I still was a JV starter, but now I was one of only two sophomores suiting up with the varsity team.

Our team wasn't half bad. I was still learning every day as Coach Larabus poured his morning wisdom into me.

I was fifteen at the time. It has been three decades since he coached me for only one season before I moved across town and away from Clarkston, but I still can hear his yell: *"You can never waste your time on the court,"* he'd say. *"When you're there, you don't ever rest. When you need rest, let me know, and I'll rest you. When you're on that court, I want everything you have. When you are worn out, just let me know. I'll sit you down for a breather, and then I'll put you back in. Leave it all on the court. Every time. You may have thirty seconds to play, but you had better spend every ounce of energy you have in those thirty seconds. You may have five minutes left. The same rule applies. Be ready to give it your all."*

He drilled that into me until I began responding in every game. That's why I found myself on varsity by midseason.

I remember one of my first varsity games. We reached the second half and the score was close. I heard Coach Larabus call my name, and his philosophy was so ingrained in me that I flew off the bench, began tearing off my warm-up suit, and sprinted to him. Our team had just come out of a huddle and was returning to the court after a time-out. I reached the coach and he looked at me like I was nuts.

"Don't take off your warm-ups," he said.

"Well, didn't you call me?"

"Yeah."

I thought he was about to send me into the game. He had other ideas.

"One of the cheerleaders left her pom poms on the court," he said. "Go get 'em."

I tried not to let my shoulders slump. I thought, *Oh, great. Now I'm the errand boy for the cheerleaders.*

Embarrassed though I was, I remembered that Coach Larabus drilled us to give maximum effort in everything we did. So I ran in a full sprint, picked up the two pom poms, ran back, looked at the coach, and asked, "Is that what you wanted?"

"Absolutely," he said.

I got to play in the next varsity game. I played maybe thirty seconds, but I played. It didn't matter if it was only picking up pom poms, I demonstrated that I had bought into his philosophy. That has carried over into every area of my life with immeasurable benefit.

I was willing to work hard. I was willing to step out of my comfort zone, even if it meant swallowing my pride to retrieve pom poms in front of a packed gymnasium. I was willing to put others before me. I was willing to submit to authority. I was willing to take advice and constructive criticism. I was willing to learn. I was willing to *earn*.

The Bible states, "It is fine to be zealous, provided the purpose is good" (Galatians 4:18) and also implores us to "never tire of doing what is right" (2 Thessalonians 3:13). Christ calls us to give our all in life.

One of my favorite quotes is good bulletin-board material:

> Excellence can be obtained if you: care more than others think is wise, risk more than others think is safe, dream more than others think is practical, expect more than others think is possible.

I cannot find who said it. I know it wasn't Coach Larabus. But it was someone like him.

Our acrostic of D-R-E-A-M has an "E" right in the middle. There is a reason. That is the letter symbolizing the element that drives everything else. It stands for "Enthusiasm," and it is the motor behind a fulfilled life. So much of your life feeds off of the big "E."

Since enthusiasm is the motor, it begs a question:

You're in one of the most important times in your life. Do you know what gear you're in?

Of all the everyday sights that I most take for granted, the grouping of the letters P-R-N-D has to be near the top of the list. I didn't realize this until recently, when my car needed servicing. I have a friend who sells cars. While his dealership serviced my car, he provided me a loaner. He was really nice to me. It was a BMW convertible.

I'd never driven a car like it. I realized just how different it was when I started the engine and grabbed the shifter, which was on the console to my right. Problem is, I had no idea of the location of the gears. There was no P-R-N-D window beside the shifter and no label on top of it. I was stumped. I kept looking around the console, trying to figure out the gear sequence before daring to take my foot off the brake.

Befuddled, I looked up. There it was. From the dash blared a digital readout so cool that it almost looked like a hologram. It was disconcerting, especially considering that the digital P-R-N-D didn't have the accompanying numbers 1–2–3 to indicate the lower gears. It just read P-R-N-D, right there on the dash. Weird.

I was so struck by the large and bold initials that I stared at them as a thought froze me.

Hmm. Park, Reverse, Neutral, and Drive. That's just the way people live their lives. Immediately, I thought about this chapter. When I languished through my teenage struggles, I could have been characterized as living in Park. Maybe you can find yourself in one of these areas:

P

People stuck in Park either don't have any desires at all or for various reasons refuse to pursue their desires. I'm not sure which is worse.

People in Park often focus only on security and familiarity. They say, "Hey, this is comfortable, and I'm just going to sit here for a while." It's almost as if they believe life is never going to change if they sit still. But everything changes daily. Life *is* change.

The sad truth for people who never leave Park is that one day they're going to face death, look back over their lives, and think, *What did I really accomplish?* Somewhere along the line, they stopped moving forward. When you meet them and ask, "Hey, how is it going?" they usually respond, "Oh, I'm just holding on. Just hanging in there."

Being parked means you've got your anchor down, you're not moving at all, and all of life is whizzing past. Rather than diving into the sweep of human history and the movement of God's plan, you're entrenched. You attempt only to hold your own.

The reason most often is fear. We'll address this in the next chapter.

R

Living in Reverse means living in the past. These folks spend their whole lives saying, "Well, I could have, but . . . If only this had happened, I would have . . . "

Their whole lives are spent with an arm propped on the passenger seat, head craning behind them to peer through the small, dusty rear window of what-could-have-been.

When I was growing up, my dad and I would go fishing in Abbeville, a tiny South Georgia mosquito bed where my grandmother lived. Our whole family would convene on the Ocmulgee River. My dad and my "uncle" always pulled up a chair together.

The scene brought a strange family twist. They had become best buddies growing up. They are double first cousins because their dads are brothers and they married girls who are sisters. So their lives are interwoven like kinfolk kudzu.

I recall sitting near the riverbank every year and listening to my dad and uncle. Invariably, the talk turned to their dreams.

"We're going to build us a house down here on the river. We're going to buy some land, build a house, and come down here all the time and fish."

They even talked about floor plans and how the family would share the time there. They had everything worked out in their minds.

That happened every year. For a while.

But after several years, I noticed that the conversation changed to past tense. They began saying things like, "Well, if we had only bought that land, we'd have this and that. If we had only . . . "

It was interesting to watch how it changed for them. They started living life in Reverse. All of their fishing trips were spent reminiscing, dwelling on the past, and lamenting what could have been. It was a great lesson for a teenager to observe.

Every October 31, our church welcomes our community to the largest fall festival in the county. Thousands of people stream onto our football field and track for rides, candy, and entertainment. Almost everyone dresses in a "happy" or fun costume. Last year, I went as Napoleon Dynamite.

Juan DeVevo, one of the guitarists for Casting Crowns and one of our youth workers, is a terrific videographer. He had filmed a takeoff of the movie *Napoleon Dynamite* for a lesson series on dating, which our student pastors, Mark Hall and Reagan Farris, presented to our youth group. I borrowed the Napoleon Dynamite costume pieces from Juan, added a few of my own, and walked around in a hideous nerd wig and a "Jesus Loves Pedro" T-shirt. With my facial features, I was a dead ringer. Some people didn't recognize me at first even though I preach to them every Sunday. They had to ask if it was me.

There are great lessons in that goofy movie. One of them is to draw an illustration from the life of Uncle Rico, who promised that "back in '82" he could throw the pigskin a quarter mile.

During the entire movie, when he's not hawking dubious products door-to-door, Uncle Rico is filming himself throwing a football. He's stuck in 1982, even though you get the sneaking suspicion that his '82 wasn't nearly as big a year as he claims. He's not moving forward. His life is a scratchy "highlight" reel from two decades earlier.

It's easy to get there from here. All you have to do is live in Park for a while. Then your shifter

P-R-N-D

almost always winds up only in the next gear down: Reverse.

The reason is usually, once again, fear.

N

While people in Park are frozen from fear, lack of confidence, or laziness, people stuck in Neutral are different—because they're indifferent. They're apathetic and noncommittal. They could go either way. They float through life, swept into the currents of the latest crowd-think. It's a dangerous—and too prevalent—way of life.

You cannot lead, you cannot govern effectively, and you cannot live courageously and productively if you go by popular opinion. That's why I always arch my eyebrows when I hear someone described as "trendy." I don't want to bone up on what's popular. I prefer having a little backbone, period. If being godly means being out of style, then that is the one way I most want to stand out from the crowd.

Being in Neutral means having no identity. It means existing in a land of perilous compromise, where whatever someone else says goes. I do want to live by what someone else says, but His name is Jesus. Nothing about Jesus was or is neutral. He just happens to be the most radical revolutionary the world has ever seen, and His Spirit living on the inside of you will make you one too.

There is a reason many people go with the flow. They don't want to stand on their own out of—you guessed it—fear.

D

At this point, you probably expect me to launch into the virtues of doing what the Ford Motor Company commercial implores us to do: "Live life in Drive."

Indeed, I encourage you to shift all the way down to D and live your life in Drive. But look first in God's glove compartment and pull out the owner's manual.

When you put your life in D, you'll begin moving. But if you don't have any direction, it doesn't matter. You can follow Ford's advice and live life in D, and your life can still be a disaster. You've got to watch where you're headed.

You can move with passion, you can be headed somewhere with enthusiasm, but that doesn't mean it's in the direction God has for you. If you're just moving for the sake of moving, nothing substantive defines your life. If it is not of God, then it has no eternal value and bears no eternal weight. It is superficial. It is the chorus of a Kansas song. It is "Dust in the Wind."

Dust in the wind obviously is driven in a direction. But where to? And for what purpose? And just look at the mess it makes.

If you are pointed in any direction other than the dream God has reserved specifically for you, then you're headed the wrong way. God can and will redeem the lost time in some way, but it's up to you to surrender and obey. Jesus said it is more blessed to give than to receive. The sole way to learn this truth and put it into practice is by dying to yourself and giving *yourself* away to Christ (Galatians 2:20; Luke 14:26–27).

The reason most people don't do this—not even believers who stream through our church doors every week—is because of our old friend . . .

Fear.

In the next chapter, though, I'd like to introduce you to another old friend who will help us make sure we stay on track.

DREAM Challenge:

Go ahead . . . be a sellout.

As I look back on my young adulthood, I remember the sense of restlessness that stirred me. I didn't know which direction to take, but I brimmed with enthusiasm. I so wanted to make a mark. I so thrived on my newfound freedom after high school. I so hungered for an identity.

But how? Where?

Enthusiasm is like charcoal. By itself, it will burn until it is nothing more than an ash heap—dust in the wind. But it becomes a source of positive energy when a nice slab of meat is added to the equation. If your life is to have meat, it must be founded on the Word of God, steeped in obedience, marked by relentless and unabashed abandonment, and totally dependent upon a holy God in an unholy world.

Is there anything keeping you from this? Is it fear?

If so, then those messages are coming from the enemy and not from God.

**For God has not given us a spirit of fear, but of power and of love and of a sound mind.
(2 Timothy 1:7 NKJV)**

You don't have to be bogged down in the sludge of indecision.

As a pastor of a Baptist church—a denomination famous for arguing over carpet color, as the old joke goes—I know how difficult it is for some people to change. Sometimes the challenge is even greater when you're young and seemingly the whole world is before you—with its many opportunities and pitfalls.

The answer is called abandonment.

Abandonment means living enthusiastically and wholeheartedly for Jesus—no apologies (sometimes you'll offend people who need to be offended when you live like this) and no reservations. Just sheer Jesus juice coursing through your veins.

As always, God's way and the world's way are at odds here. In the world, being a sellout has a negative connotation. It means you have prostituted yourself. But in God's economy, being a sellout means everything. In fact, it's the only way to fulfillment.

The Lord's timing is always perfect. An old "friend" of mine is Oswald Chambers. You would do well to purchase a copy of his daily devotional book *My Utmost for His Highest.* This morning, before I sat down to write this chapter, I was reading in his devotional about whether we are prepared to surrender totally to Christ and let go.

The true test of abandonment or surrender is in refusing to say, "Well, what about this?" Beware of your own ideas and speculations. The moment you allow yourself to think, "What about this?" you show that you have not surrendered and that you do not really trust God. But once you do surrender, you will no longer think about what God is going to do. Abandonment means to refuse yourself the luxury of asking any questions. If you totally abandon yourself to God, He immediately says to you, "I will give your life to you as a prize. . . ." The reason people are tired of life is that God has not given them anything—they have not been given their life "as a prize." The way to get out of that condition is to abandon yourself to God.[1]

My challenge is this: If your life is worth living, then it's worth living all the way. A partial commitment is no commitment at all. There is no better life to live, there's not a better journey to take, there's not a better dream to chase (indeed, it's the only *true* dream) than the one God has designed for you—if you'll just give it your all. Not a half effort or partial effort. Not making Him a part of your life. But allowing Him to *be* your life.

The construction foreman of comfort zones is Mr. Fear. The Great Unknown is an abyss for many. Jesus asks that you step into it and see what happens. He won't make you. He just asks. He invites. It's conditional. He opens with one simple word—

If . . .

If anyone would come after me, he must deny himself and take up his cross and follow me. For whoever wants to save his life will lose it, but whoever loses his life for me will find it. What good will it be for a man if he gains the whole world, yet forfeits his soul? Or what can a man give in exchange for his soul? (Matthew 16:24–26)

When you are a child of God, you don't have to fear anymore. You can live and move and have your being in God because you are His child and own all of the rights thereof. And once you're His, you'll always be His. The apostle Paul instructed the believers in Rome not to worry about the intense persecution around them "because those who are led by the Spirit of God are sons of God. For you did not receive a spirit that makes you a slave again to *fear*, but you received the Spirit of sonship" (Romans 8:14–15, *emphasis added*).

If you will only believe this truth and act accordingly, fear will evaporate. Greater is He who is in you than he who is in the world (1 John 4:4). So go ahead . . . be a sellout. Let that simmering cauldron of enthusiasm erupt into fervor for life and for the Lord of life.

After all, the old adage is true. Life is too short. Even the Bible says so . . .

"Whatever your hand finds to do, do it with all your might, for in the grave, where you are going, there is neither working nor planning nor knowledge nor wisdom" (Ecclesiastes 9:10).

In the grave, it's too late to give it your all. You're done. Reward or judgment is next.

So get going in God's direction. And go with everything you've got. You'll find that the Great Unknown is not an abyss but an adventure.

Dare you take the plunge? The Lord Jesus is there, waiting. He will help you every step of the way—

If . . .

DREAM Resolution:

I surrender to the Lord my fear in the following areas:

_____

_____

_____

_____

_____

_____

I pledge to be a sellout in the following ways:

_____

_____

_____

_____

_____

_____

aspirations

Fifty Bucks' Worth of Wisdom

People are just people.

Whether we are on skid row or in the front row at church, people are people. We're made in the image of God and can be brilliant, impossibly loving, and irrationally forgiving, but we're also fallible and maddeningly inconsistent and inconsiderate. We're so focused on ourselves that the attention we give others pales in comparison. Others get our leftovers.

This is why Jesus gave us the two greatest commandments.

"Love the Lord your God with all your heart and with all your soul and with all your mind." This is the first and greatest commandment. And the second is like it: "Love your neighbor as yourself." All the Law and the Prophets hang on these two commandments. (Matthew 22:37–40)

Our aspirations—the strong desires we have to excel and achieve—naturally turn inward. Most people's aspirations are not others-centered. They're self-centered. This is why so many people are unfulfilled and lament over falling short of their goals.

The Bible tells us that we are not created to live for ourselves. We're designed to live for God. If we are made in His image and He is others-focused, then the only path to contentment is to live for Him and for others, just as He does. God lives for himself. He's God, so He has that privilege. He has designed the entire universe to sing His praises and to reflect glory upon Him because He alone is worthy of honor. Yet He also lives for others, and He sent His Son to die for others.

He asks us to do the same—to live and die for Him and for others. I was already a minister before this truth really hit home.

One of my first paid jobs in ministry was as a part-time youth pastor at Pleasant Hill Baptist Church in fast-growing Gwinnett County outside of Atlanta. It was 1982 (right about the time Uncle Rico was throwing the pigskin a quarter-mile), and I led the youth ministry while pursuing my college degree. I made fifty dollars a week for about thirty hours of work.

That's why it's called ministry.

A man in the church provided a little furnished apartment in an older area of town, and I was thrilled to have it for free. I had worked for about a year when the church began preparing its annual budget.

It was a typical Wednesday night business meeting. They eventually addressed personnel and were looking at salaries when they came to my name.

The pastor had submitted a request to raise my salary to seventy-five dollars a week with a twenty-five-dollar car allowance. As soon as I was mentioned, a lady on the committee stood and turned toward me.

"I'd like to ask our student pastor to leave so we can talk honestly about this," she said. "I'd also like to ask his girlfriend [now my wife, Christie] and her parents to leave."

The pastor, who chaired the committee, thought such a small request would sail through approval. He expressed mild dismay at the suggestion but asked us to step out.

So Christie, her parents, and I shuffled out the door. No problem. I'd just wait outside for five minutes and get my smile ready to return and accept my raise.

Sure enough, five minutes later, the doors opened. I headed toward the door when the pastor stepped out.

"You ready for us to go back in?" I asked.

"No, I've got to stay out too."

"Why do you have to stay out?"

"Well, I hired you. They said I would interfere with the discussion, so they wanted me to remove myself."

The chairman of the deacons, a man named Alvin, took over the business meeting. Pretty soon the door opened again, and Alvin stepped out. He wasn't there to call us back inside either. The committee had asked him to leave too. He had two kids in the student ministry, and since he was one of my adult workers in the ministry, they thought he would bias the conversation.

More than an hour later, we were still sitting outside the room, staring at the door handle.

I couldn't fathom what was so controversial about a twenty-five-dollar salary raise and twenty-five-dollar car allowance. I admit that the debate got under my skin. I decided to go home.

I stopped by my office, sat at my desk, and reflected upon what was going on across the building. I didn't understand it. I was young and full of vigor—sometimes too full. I made an emotional decision.

You know what? This really isn't worth it. I'm in college. I'm working my tail off. The student ministry is growing. This aggravation, this lack of appreciation, isn't worth it.

I grabbed a sheet of the church's letterhead and scribbled a note to the pastor: *"If these people want $50 a week that badly, they can keep the other $50. I resign."*

I signed and dated it, folded it, and placed it on the pastor's desk. I walked out and drove back to my apartment. I was done. I would become a full-time student.

An hour later Christie's father and the pastor knocked on my door. They began trying to talk me out of resigning.

"First off," the pastor said, "you're going to set the church up for problems. They're going to say, 'Hey, we got him on that one; we'll get him on something else too.' They'll dominate this church."

But that's not what changed my mind, sad as it was. Something else did. He asked me a series of questions.

"Who are you working for? Are you working for me? Are you working for the church? Or are you working for the Lord? Better yet, who are you *living* for?"

I stood there, speechless. He could not have had more impact on me had he hit me with his fist. I wasn't ready for it.

All along, God had been working in my life, drawing me ever closer to the fulfillment of what I'd heard in my home stairway as an eighteen-year-old. I had the vision. It was just focused on the wrong person.

After my pastor's words peeled the scales from my eyes, only a few moments passed before I squinted and mustered a new resolve.

"Okay, you're right," I said. "Because I'm not working for you, for me, or even for the church. I'm working for Jesus."

Soon after, they passed the salary increase. By the time I eventually moved on, the student ministry had quadrupled in size. As if confirming that He had worked through me, the Lord replaced me with one of my former students, who led the student ministry to even greater heights. The people who had balked at my raise ended up leaving the church.

I learned that ambition, essential and inspiring, also can be wrong-headed. And wrong-hearted. Even in the Lord's work—*especially* in the Lord's work— you must check your motives. Philippians 2:3–4 is a superb motive manager:

Do nothing out of selfish ambition or vain conceit, but in humility consider others better than yourselves. Each of you should look not only to your own interests, but also to the interests of others.

There will be times when you wonder whether the cost is too great, just as I did when I spelled out my disgust in the resignation letter. There will be times when the world's sway seems too strong to resist. That's when you should squint and muster a new resolve.

On the heels of the section on Enthusiasm, you may ask, "Well, is it worth giving my full effort?"

Yes, yes, a lifetime of yes.

There is a reason you hear the statements, "If it's worth doing, it's worth doing right," and, "If it's not worth doing right, it's not worth doing at all." It's because, regardless of what you're doing—whether you're working in construction or as a teacher, banker, accountant, or student—you should live for Jesus. Aspire to greatness *in Him*. It's worth it only because of Him.

Don't ask, "Is it worth giving my all?" Instead, the proper question is, "Is *He* worth giving my all?"

Regardless of our task, our station, or our budding aspirations, the object of our affection is Jesus and the goal of that affection is His glory. If we are living for anything else, we substitute our will for God's will. We replace the dream for a scheme.

And while people are just people, we will see in Psalm 91 how God's way is so much better.

The Seven Wills of God

Have you ever noticed that you seem to want whatever you keep an eye on? You want what you watch.

So I encourage you to watch what you want.

I'm not recommending that you eyeball whatever you wish. Just the opposite. "Watch what you want" is a southern way to encourage caution toward objects of your focus and affection. Guard your desires and make sure they are rooted in Scripture. Aspirations and achievements are good when centered upon Christ and His will for you. They are dangerous when fueled by the flesh—as I learned in my fifty-dollar salary flap.

So "watch what you want." You will want what you watch.

Early in 1994 Sid Callaway, the director for our area chapter of the Fellowship of Christian Athletes, called me about an upcoming FCA breakfast during the festivities for Super Bowl XXVIII in Atlanta. The Dallas Cowboys were preparing to play the Buffalo Bills in the Georgia Dome, and the FCA used the opportunity to reach athletes and raise funds.

"Hey, why don't you bring Micah down and meet all these Georgia players and Joe Gibbs and Jay Barker?" Sid asked.

My son, Micah, was six years old and loved sports. I jumped at the chance to get him in the same room with several players from the University of Georgia and Georgia Tech.

The two featured speakers were Coach Joe Gibbs, who was more than a year into his first retirement after leaving the Washington Redskins, and Jay Barker, who had quarterbacked the University of Alabama to the national championship in a stunning upset of the University of Miami in the Sugar Bowl one year earlier.

I thought the highlight of the day would be when Georgia offensive lineman Adam Meadows volunteered to sign Micah's UGA hat and then escorted him to get all of the Bulldogs' autographs. Micah walked back to his seat beaming.

Joe Gibbs was a wonderful speaker as he shared about how his faith helped him build a franchise that won three Super Bowls. But I never would have guessed that in a room full of stars, superstars, and world-class coaches, a smallish, handsome Alabama boy would make the biggest impression.

I still remember almost everything Jay Barker said.

Jay grew up in Alabama and always dreamed of going to the University of Alabama to follow in the footsteps of great Crimson Tide quarterbacks like Joe Namath and Ken Stabler. He set that as his goal.

After a great high-school career, Jay was recruited by several colleges, including Alabama. He finally signed with his dream school and fulfilled a lifelong ambition.

So he had to set another goal. His next priority was to become Alabama's starting quarterback.

After being redshirted his first year, Jay eventually won the starting job just as he had envisioned. It was time to set another goal. He decided he'd like to be known as the quarterback who led the Tide to another Southeastern Conference championship. When his sophomore season rolled around, he did just that. Mission accomplished.

Now what?

Jay decided the only remaining goal was a national championship, which would be the twelfth in Alabama's storied history. Making the quest even greater was that he was playing for Gene Stallings, a fine Christian man and a disciple of legendary coach Paul "Bear" Bryant.

Next came the Sugar Bowl and Alabama's victory over heavily favored Miami. Afterward, Jay was exuberant. He had played brilliantly, 'Bama was the national champion, and every dream Jay had ever conceived had come to pass. The hoopla back in Alabama was even more chaotic.

During his FCA speech, Jay recalled returning home to the celebration parade, where everyone adored him and snapped photos of him holding the

NCAA trophy. It was a bigger response than even he had imagined.

After the celebration, Jay Barker returned home, sat alone, and looked around. In the hush, it hit him.

"Is that it?" he asked himself. "There has to be more to life than this."

I'm paraphrasing now, but Jay went on to tell what he learned: "Whatever goals and ambitions that you set in life are temporal. Whenever you reach them you're going to find out that, in and of themselves, they're empty. Your whole life, your desires, and your ambitions need to be to live for Jesus. You can pursue things, but pursue them while living for Jesus."

All these years later, his reminders resonate with me. I was pastor of a young but growing church when I heard him speak, and his words pierced me. I thought, *Wow, that's interesting—that you have to watch what you desire, because your desires can take you away from Jesus as well as take you to Him. You can be living for the wrong goals.*

Then I remembered the same lesson from my fifty-dollar pay raise. Pastors, athletes, actors, construction workers, and homemakers all can live for the wrong goals.

Just recently, one of our student pastors, Reagan Farris, told me he watched talented actor Anthony Hopkins accept an award on television. Reagan was caught off guard when Hopkins stood at the microphone and said, in effect, "This is nice, but there has to be more."

I was struck by his sentiments too. That's hardly the philosophy of most Hollywood types. So I visited a Web site on Hopkins to check whether he had made similar comments before, and I found this quote from him:

"I know that in the end there is a peace, a real peace, and maybe darkness and nothing. I don't have morbid thoughts about it. My epitaph if I ever have one will be, 'What was all that about?' "

Here is an Academy Award winner who also has won the Golden Globe for Lifetime Achievement, and yet he says his own epitaph will read: "What was all that about?"

Wow.

That's a pretty empty life.

The point is this: Guard your desires. Let your desires be shaped by God in every area of your life. Scripture warns us about our desires, whether they are for money, fame, sex, or status. Guard your heart and mind, and know that even the disciples struggled in this area (Mark 9:33–37). Unless your desires are rooted in Christ, it's not a matter of *if* they will take you down the wrong road but *when*.

God's Word isn't a killjoy, however. It doesn't discourage us from dreaming. It inspires us to dream—and to dream grandly. Go after life with every morsel of your being, but let your desires be shaped by God.

The old adage that says, "Be careful what you wish for—you may just get it" is never truer than in the spiritual realm.

King David told the Lord in Psalm 40:8, "I desire to do your will, O my God; your law is within my heart."

So how do we determine God's will? It is a struggle common to every believer. How do we know whether our Decisions, Relationships, Enthusiasm, Aspirations, and Mission are within God's will?

I appreciate an approach taught by the Christian ministry Stand to Reason, which encourages people struggling to determine God's will to consider three areas:

- **God's Moral Will—What does Scripture say?** We learn God's moral will through reading, careful consideration, diligent study, research, asking questions, meditation, memorization, and gifted teachers.

- **Wisdom—Have I prayed for wisdom?** We gain wisdom through prayer, counsel, instruction, research, and experience.

- **Personal Factors—What are my personal thoughts?** In any decision, we should examine our desires, abilities, and consciences. Overarching all of this is God's sovereignty. He is in control, which should give us freedom and rest.[1]

Follow the leading of the Holy Spirit as you plan. And remember that His first name is *Holy.*

Finally, step out in faith and believe the Lord's pledges in Psalm 91. During most of this beautiful passage, the psalmist speaks of the security of an intimate walk with God. The last three verses (14–16 NKJV) are the Lord's own words, however.

Because he has set his love upon Me, therefore I will deliver him; I will set him on high, because he has known My name. He shall call upon Me, and I will answer him; I will be with him in trouble; I will deliver him and honor him. With long life I will satisfy him, and [I will] show him My salvation.

Notice the seven "wills" of God in this passage. Even when we don't know where we're going or what we're doing, when we struggle to find God's will, He has our best in mind. As long as we abide in Him (John 15:1–11), He promises to show us the flip side of His will:

- **God WILL rescue you:** Nothing is too dire to keep you from God's reach.
- **God WILL protect you:** When you're walking with the Lord and acknowledging Him, you dwell in His "shelter," or "secret place" (see

verse 1 of Psalm 91). There, the enemy cannot touch you.

- **God WILL answer you:** God is faithful to give you the best answer every time, and many times His "no" is the best answer.

- **God WILL be with you in trouble:** Hebrews 13:5 promises that God will never leave you nor forsake you, no matter what.

- **God WILL deliver you and honor you:** His deliverance isn't just fire insurance. God lavishes grace and blessings on His faithful because He promises abundant life (John 10:10).

- **God WILL satisfy you with long life:** How long is eternity?

- **God WILL show you His salvation:** God's beloved children are always safe in the arms of His love; you did nothing to earn His salvation, and you can do nothing to cause Him to take it away (John 10:27–30; Romans 8:38–39; Ephesians 1:13–14). This truth should free you to live not for your own pursuits but for His.

These are God's promises. Now it's time to make a few of your own.

DREAM Challenge:

Keep the change.

In the first chapter of this section on Aspirations, I shared the story of my controversial pay raise as a student pastor and offered you the fifty dollars' worth of wisdom I gleaned from that ordeal.

Now I'd like you to keep the change.

I love stories of radical change, because such transformation is the hallmark of Jesus Christ. Whatever He touches changes.

One of our operations workers, Darrell Jenkins, was saved on a Sunday when our church did not have power due to an ice storm. He was a drug user who had been living in a refrigerator box. Yet God picked a date on His providential calendar and appointed Darrell to be in our church for an abbreviated service that featured music with a piano and one tuba player. He heard a twenty-minute Gospel presentation and walked down the aisle and straight into eternal life. Now he works on our staff and can hardly talk about Jesus without crying.

God offered His priceless gift, and Darrell has kept the change.

In the Bible, there are several stories of such transformation. Matthew was a despised tax collector before

Jesus gazed at him with a look of love he had never seen, and said, "Follow me." Mary Magdalene was a vessel of hell's demons until Jesus spoke them gone. The man blind since birth stood before the elite and with the simplicity of a child of God said, "All I know is I was blind but now I see."

The rich young ruler of Luke 18 and Simon the Sorcerer of Acts 8 are examples of people who flirt with Jesus but ultimately opt for their own way of life. They prefer to keep their treasures.

So if you're one of His, keep the change.

In the Old Testament, we see how the Israelites waffled between faithfulness and rebellion, blessing and discipline, abundance and hardship—just like so many of us today. Sometimes it's difficult to stay on the straight and narrow. Jesus was right. Few people enter the narrow gate because the path is so trying (Matthew 7:13–14).

But it's the only way to blessing and protection. It's the only way to provision. And most important, it's the only way to honor God.

Keep the change.

The world will beckon at every turn, but keep the change. Your flesh will crave your pet sins, but resist the devil, and he will flee from you. Keep the change.

Choose which is more important to you . . .

Jesus or your friends.

Jesus or your boyfriend.

Jesus or your girlfriend.

Jesus or your wallet.

Jesus or your good time.

Jesus or your . . . self.

While it is true that God chose you, died for you, gave you the gift of faith, and sealed you with His Holy Spirit until the day of redemption, there is also something called obedience. This submission proves whether you're truly saved. It is the litmus test of eternal life. If you are unable to live a life worthy of Christ, then you're not saved (1 John 2:3–6). However, not one hound of hell can derail you if you're truly saved. He who has the Son of God has life, but he who does not have the Son of God does not have life (1 John 5:12).

There are many verses that speak of persevering in your faith. One of the apostle Paul's favorite exhortations to believers was to "hold fast." He repeatedly urged believers to hold fast to their faith, which would prove they belonged to Jesus (1 Corinthians 15:1–2; 1 Thessalonians 5:21; 2 Thessalonians 2:15; Hebrews 3:6; Revelation 3:11).

Do you want to live within the will of God? Do you want your aspirations to lie squarely within His plans for you?

Do you want to live the dream?

Then remember this verse: "Delight yourself in the Lord and he will give you the desires of your heart" (Psalm 37:4). Many people misuse this verse as a license to "claim" material wealth. This verse simply means that when you delight in Jesus and seek after His heart, your desires will be His desires. Everything else—everything—is superficial and self-ish. At the deepest core of your life, you should be willing to say, "No matter what, I want what the Lord wants for me."

Some folks are unwilling to place this verse in context. Look at the two verses surrounding it:

"Trust in the Lord and do good" (verse 3) and "commit your way to the Lord" (verse 5).

To trust in the Lord and do good and to commit your way to the Lord require acts of the will. It means making a choice. It means obedience. It means true surrender. It means submission. It means traveling the narrow, difficult path. It means you must do one thing.

Keep the change.

DREAM Resolution:

I will work on the following areas to ensure I keep the change:

_____

_____

_____

_____

_____

_____

    I pledge to keep the change even though it may mean:

_____

_____

_____

_____

_____

_____

mission

Nudged

I stood at the bottom of the steps, staring at a little blue dot in the middle of a black screen.

Maybe you don't know what that means. That means the power was off. Television screens used to be illuminated by fuses that, when the TV was turned off, would slowly dim into a tiny blue dot that disappeared into the blackness of the screen.

So if the power was off, then why did I have goose bumps?

Seconds earlier, in the most monumental moment of my life, I heard someone address me. I had wondered for months what I was going to do with my life. I had moped. I had mulled. I had bordered on giving up. Finally, that afternoon I had prayed—if you want to call it a prayer.

But when I came home from working at McDonald's that special night years ago, I saw Billy Graham peer through the TV set and ask me, point-blank: "Do you know what God wants you to do with your life?"

I had smarted off and eventually headed to bed. That's when I heard another voice.

It didn't come from Billy Graham. I checked to make sure I had turned off the TV. What I heard on my stairway as I eased closer to my bedroom door would change my life.

It was God.

"You need to serve me. You need to be a pastor."

I heard it, sensed it, clear as a new day. I can't say it was audible, although it seemed like it was. Still, the impression was strong enough—loud enough—that I stopped on the steps. It was so comical that such a thought had entered my mind that I think I laughed aloud. At the same time, I was stunned. I couldn't dismiss it, so I returned downstairs again to double-check the TV.

That's when I was left alone with my goose bumps at the bottom of the stairs.

I thought, *Man, I don't know why I'm thinking about that. Good grief. There's no way I can pastor a church.* I went upstairs and went to bed, a little spooked, a lot puzzled, and completely unaware that the God of all the universe had just reached from His throne and nudged me on the shoulder.

He had just given me my dream.

The next day, I tried to ignore the thought and went back to work. It was no use. As I stood there and flipped burgers, I couldn't shake what I had experienced. Over and over I sensed the same directive: *"You need to preach. You need to serve me."* The message was never audible. It was much louder than that. I had never experienced such passion before— the closest I had come was in basketball. Now this was getting all of my attention.

I remember thinking, *This is just weird. What am I going to tell people? "Hey, I think God is calling me to preach"?* They would laugh to hear me, of all people, say that. I wasn't exactly sure what was going on, and I didn't know what to do with it.

For the next four weeks, I tried to put aside the thought, but it wouldn't leave me alone. I had completed my course requirements in high school and was awaiting graduation. My daily routine consisted of working at McDonald's and playing pickup basketball games. Still, nothing altered God's impression upon me. Everywhere I went, my gut churned with the same instruction. I said to myself, *"I don't even know what that means or what to do, but I need to do what He says."*

Finally, I did what every hardened, newly independent young man does when he gets in a bind.

I went to Momma.

I walked into the kitchen where she was preparing a meal and cleared my throat.

"Mom, do you remember when you told me to pray about what I'm supposed to do with my life?"

"Yes. Have you been doing it?"

"Actually, I did it once."

"Well?"

"I think God wants me to preach."

"What?!"

I fidgeted. "I don't know. I think He wants me to become a pastor."

The shock on her face begged the question *Is this my son?*

I told my dad that night. He was an accountant, so he was a detail-oriented, analytical type. He loved Jesus, though, and was faithful in service. He listened and advised me the way any good accountant and dad would.

"You know, maybe this is what God is telling you to do," he said, "but you probably need to go to college to get a business degree or something just in case you need something to fall back on."

In other words, he was thinking, *Tim may be reaching for something to do because he doesn't know what to do.* Had I been in his shoes, I would've had the same reaction. My announcement came out of nowhere and surprised him.

Well, maybe he's right, I thought, and tried to forget about it. I was tired of obsessing about the preacher stuff. I wanted to move on. A college degree in any field would be a wonderful "something to fall back on."

Dad helped me get accepted to Georgia Southern, which is where I would pursue an accounting degree.

I was enjoying my last summer before leaving for college when I had another breakthrough. I had been trying to overlook God's calling on my life, but my mental gymnastics weren't working. It was like holding up an umbrella at Niagara Falls. Even the underside gets wet.

I had started a daily Bible study after God spoke to me in the stairway, and for the first time in my life I was maintaining it. One day I was in my room, reading through the Gospels. I don't know what I was looking for, just something—anything—that would provide more direction. I'm not sure I was absorbing anything when another thought struck me.

Fall back on? I need something to fall back on? God, is that insulting?

Emotionally spent, I stopped and prayed, "Okay, God, I'm pretty miserable right now, so if that's what you want me to do—become a pastor—I'll do it . . . with nothing to fall back on."

It was Wednesday, which was perfect timing. I decided to go to that night's church service and respond during the invitation. I would walk down front and tell the pastor that God was calling me to preach.

I didn't reveal my intentions for the evening, not even to my parents. I simply made up my mind to go on my own.

I had just turned eighteen. I got into my car and placed my Bible in the passenger seat. I still looked like a hippie, so I wondered how my announcement would go over at our small Baptist church. I backed out of the driveway and drove maybe five hundred yards from my house when I glanced in my rearview mirror.

Blue lights.

This was new territory for me. Already tense with anticipation, my heart was now lodged somewhere near my voice box. Maybe that's why I sounded so high-pitched when I answered the police officer.

He was training a rookie officer. So there I was in my jacked-up Chevelle featuring ultra-loud headers, mag wheels, and wide back tires. I looked like something out of "Born to Be Wild," which meant I was an alluring target for a patrolman. He walked to my window and asked for my license.

"Yes, sir," I said, fumbling through my wallet.

"Where do you think you're going?"

"I'm going to church."

These are his exact words: "Boy, now is not the time to get smart."

"No sir, I really am. It's Wednesday night, and I'm going to church. Here's my Bible."

"Don't show me your daddy's Bible, boy."

Of course, the rookie was there, soaking in every pulsating, by-the-book syllable. I realized I was in trouble because Barney was deputizing Goober, and there was no way he wasn't going to make a point. I just didn't know what his point was.

The officer saw that my license was legit and up-to-date. Then he told me why he had stopped me.

"Do you realize you have an expired inspection sticker?"

"No, sir," I squeaked. My sticker had expired two months earlier. Amid my young adult wilderness experience, I had forgotten to renew it.

The officer looked at me with a confidence that he already knew the answer as he asked a second time, "So, where are you going?"

"To church."

"Wrong answer."

"Okay. What's the right answer?"

"To get your car inspected."

"Oh. Yes, sir. That's where I'm going."

He smirked.

"You know what? I don't believe anything coming out of your mouth," he said. "I'll tell you what we're going to do. We're going to follow you home. You're going to park this car until tomorrow morning. And tomorrow morning, the first thing you're going to do is drive it to the inspection station. I'm going to write you a warning."

Only a warning. I was relieved.

I was on my way to tell the church that God had called me to preach when I was pulled over by a policeman for the first time in my life. He followed me into our driveway. I thought he would go to our door to talk to my parents, but he stayed in his car and leaned out the window.

"Tomorrow morning. First thing. I'm going to be watching you."

I was shaking. I went inside and told Dad the story and asked to borrow his truck. He handed me the keys, happy that I was headed to church on my own.

When I reached the church, I found a vacant pew and sat alone. I wasn't interested in sitting with buddies. I don't remember a thing the preacher said. I could focus only on the inspirational pull of God and the fear smothering my eighteen-year-old heart.

I was petrified of walking to the altar at the conclusion of the service. I had accepted Christ as my personal Savior while at the beach when I was eleven, so I had never really walked alone to the front of a church during invitation time.

The moment finally arrived. I rose to my feet, my pulse pounding in my temples, and eased into the aisle. It felt as if every eye in the room bore down upon me. I approached the pastor, ready to surrender, ready to give my life, my career, my all to Jesus, ready to stun the congregation, rattle the world, and invoke the voices of angels . . .

Only to get the same reaction from my pastor that I had received from my mom.

"Hey, I just wanted to tell you that I've been called to preach."

I think his eyes widened before he caught himself.

"Are you sure?" he asked.

Let the angels sing!

Those were his exact words: "Are you sure?" He seemed taken aback.

In retrospect I don't blame him, because I was the kid in the youth group about whom everyone would've said, "He's not really committed. He's here all the time because his dad and mom are here, but he's not serious."

The pastor rebounded quickly. Everyone was watching, after all.

"Okay, sit here on the front pew and fill this out."

I filled out the church's form before the pastor stood me in front of the congregation and put his arm around me.

"This young man in our church, you all know him. He's been coming with his parents, who are members here. He tells me that God has called him to preach, so we need to pray for him."

Everybody came by and shook my hand and told me how excited they were for me. I wonder how many of them were saying to themselves, "Yeah, right." After the service, the pastor looked at me and said, "I would like to talk more with you. Come by and see me."

That was fine by me. I didn't know what to do next anyway. When I met with him, he wanted to gauge my commitment. "Are you sure God has called you to preach?" he asked again. "Let's make sure that this is really what needs to happen."

The whole time, I couldn't help but think: *He and my dad have talked.*

Now that I'm older, I realize they probably had not talked but were suffering from shock and healthy skepticism. At the time, it left me less than inspired to become the next great evangelist. Now I realize that the pastor knew if he could talk me out of this step, then God hadn't really called me to take it.

As the hazy summer seeped toward fall, the pastor tried to work with me before I entered college to major in accounting. I began waffling again. It didn't take long before I was muttering to myself, "You know, God probably wouldn't have called me to preach. I mean, look at me. I'm a preacher?"

So I went to college and focused on accounting and had an easy time because it came naturally to me. During my freshman year, there were several days in which our professor had to leave. She asked me to teach the class for her. It was just that easy. Everything in accounting made sense, and nothing in this "call-of-God" thing made any sense at all.

I looked at my accounting grades and thought, *Well, maybe I am supposed to do this.*

Maybe God got it wrong. Or maybe I didn't *really* hear from Him. Maybe Dad was right after all.

Maybe I needed something to fall back on.

You don't have a mission. God does. You weren't designed to undertake your own mission. You were designed for His.

The question you face is whether you'll fall in step with His mission or insist on going it alone in this world to "make your mark." The person in lockstep with Jesus is on the only mission worth pursuing, the only real mission that exists.

If you want to see passion, watch the television show *American Inventor*. Many of the aspiring inventors on the program are consumed by their quests to produce the next great product. Some of them have sold their homes to finance their projects. One lady who was weary of broken locks on stall doors in public rest rooms invented a gizmo that fits atop the doors to ensure they remained closed while occupied. It looked as if it would cost about fifty cents in plastic to manufacture. Yet she told the judges that her greatest desire was to see her product hit the market so that she would have left a mark in the world.

Well, the bathroom stall may be occupied, but the ambition is empty.

I'm not minimizing a well-meaning woman's efforts to improve potty breaks, but I do believe we should aim to leave an *eternal* imprint.

The Bible calls man's life a vapor. We're here and gone so quickly. Since that is the case, what lasting reward is there for any effort that does not glorify God and build His kingdom? If man be but a mist though he is God's highest creation, what is our puny self-service?

If it doesn't have God's stamp of approval, it is wasted effort. It's wood, hay, and stubble. God's Word states that every believer will face a judgment to try his life's fruit as by fire. If the labor is of God, the fire will refine it just as it does gold, silver, and precious stones. The believer will enjoy reward. However, if it is of the flesh, the fire will consume it just as it does wood, hay, and stubble (1 Corinthians 3:10–15 KJV). All that is left is a pile of worthless ashes.

God's mission for us is summarized in two passages of Scripture: 1) the two greatest commandments (Matthew 22:34–40) spelled out in the previous section on Aspirations, and 2) the Great Commission (Matthew 28:18–20).

Both of these passages are direct quotes from Jesus. How does your life measure up against His mission?

I once taught a men's class on Sunday nights in which the conversation turned to priorities. I asked the men to write down their priorities, in order, from one to five. Most of the guys produced lists like this:

PRIORITIES
1. **God**
2. **Wife and kids**
3. **Friends**
4. **Career**
5. **Hobbies**

I walked up to the board and circled the first entry, which read "God." Then I drew a line from that circle to the space in front of the word PRIORITIES atop the list. In that space, I wrote "GOD'S." Our lives should be ordered by God's priorities, not our own.

The room fell silent. You could almost hear them swallow.

～

If you're going to be on a mission for God, it requires the exact opposite action than the world encourages. The world insists that you grab life by the throat, run over whatever or whoever stands in your way, and take control.

Jesus says surrender. Give up. Let go.

Perhaps man's greatest struggle is to surrender control. His second greatest struggle is to submit to someone else's authority. Jesus asks us to do both. Not just once in a while, but every day.

While floundering to find my way as a young adult, I discovered two truths about being on mission with the Lord:

- You should never have anything underneath you.
- You will always have something in front of you.

Let me illustrate.

Instead of heeding God's call to become a minister, I heeded the advice of my dad and everyone else to "have something to fall back on." I quickly discovered that God doesn't like our safety nets. They're woven by self-sufficiency.

My accounting classes left me numb. I was bored and didn't want to do it for a living. I remember thinking, *Well, if I'm not going to preach and I'm not going to be an accountant, what am I going to be?*

Notice that my mindset was still off-target. I was equating a career with what I was going "to be." A career is what you do. It's not who you are.

So I continued to run from God. Problem is, He's quick. And He never gets winded.

I became so confused that I decided to become a pilot. The television commercials looked adventuresome, so I signed up for Officer Candidate School with the Marines. I traveled to Quantico, Virginia, for training. The original plan was to attend OCS for six weeks, two straight summers, and enter the Marines as a second lieutenant when I graduated from college.

I knew I was out of place within the first week. We had a Bible study and the group leader talked about being obedient to God. I suffered intense conviction the entire time. No one else knew what God was calling me to do, but with a great degree of finality I sat there and thought, *Okay, He is not going to let me get away from this.*

Later, I had a convenient excuse to gracefully exit OCS. My knees were killing me, and the doctor told me I was ruining them. I took a medical discharge, but only after God had performed some heart surgery.

Head buzzed and shoulders slumped, I raised a white flag heavenward.

Okay, God. I'm done with running. I've been through one year of college and tried accounting. That wasn't it. I tried OCS to become a pilot, and that wasn't it. I get it now. I'll do it your way.

I didn't go back to Georgia Southern. I transferred to Mercer University in Atlanta. I was smarting spiritually because I had tried to establish Plan B in case the preaching thing didn't pan out. Now I was willing to obey the Lord because I had seen the futility of the Dowdy dream. I would try God's instead.

I told myself, "Hey, I don't need anything to fall back on. I just need to be committed to what God is calling me to do."

Safety Net

Even my dad saw my resolve and knew God's call was real. And though I would still encounter a few doubts, there was no going back. A corner was turned.

~

Having something underneath you, a safety net, reveals a lack of trust. Having something in front of you often means you are truly walking with Jesus.

Show me an effective saint, and I'll show you a strained one. Nothing intended for God's kingdom comes without challenge. The unholy trinity of the world, the flesh, and the devil will not allow easy pickings. The most effective ministries are the ones that are most attacked.

No need to fear. The Holy Trinity already is victorious (Colossians 2:13–15). The God of all grace will perfect, establish, strengthen, and settle you (1 Peter 5:10). When you face opposition, take it as a blessing. It just means you're rankling the devil. Use it as fuel. May it spur you onward. But be forewarned. When you're living for Jesus and impacting this world for His glory, you will face opposition.

Sometimes the hindrances are even comical.

Once I became a pastor, a search committee from another church visited my church to hear me preach. The eight members of the committee sat in a pew together. The pews in our old building weren't bolted to the floor. When the congregation rose to sing, the eight members of the search committee pulled themselves up by grabbing the back of the pew in front of them. By that time, the people in the front pew already were standing. The pew toppled backward into their laps and knocked them backward to overturn their own pew. We didn't raise hands much in worship that day, but there were sixteen legs in the air.

I wasn't invited to take over their pastorate.

Early on, there were other times I had to laugh to keep from crying.

My life transformed when I finally surrendered and began to major in religious studies at Mercer. I had no experience in ministry, so I had to start from scratch.

I was still a student when I was asked to preach at my church for the first time. I was so nervous that my rehearsed thirty-minute sermon shrank to only thirteen and a half minutes in the Sunday night service when I went into Alvin, Theodore, and Simon mode. I sounded like the Chipmunks.

Later, I was invited to preach at First Baptist Church of Lovejoy, Georgia. I preached on a Sunday night, and there were probably twenty-five people there. I wore a black corduroy suit.

In Georgia.

In mid-summer.

Maybe it was because I was suffocating in the suit, but as I pulled into the church parking lot, I ran over a black cat. The little girl who owned the cat witnessed its demise. Frantic, she bolted home screaming, "He killed my cat! He killed my cat!"

I opened my car door and sat on the edge of my seat and thought, *Okay, this is not working out too well. This is not a great start.*

I was still too green to realize that there will always be challenges for the faithful. There will always be something in front of you. Sometimes it's even a black cat.

Discouraged, I once again wondered if I truly had heard from God.

"This is so stupid," I muttered to myself. "I'm never going to be able to do this."

Never say never to God. He specializes in destroying absolutes. It wasn't long after I had spoken in frustration that the Lord closed the deal.

DREAM Challenge:

It's your life. Consume it or invest it.

Before you existed, there was God. Before there was an earth, there was God. Before there was a universe to hold the earth, there was God.

There is no such thing as before there was God.

The Twenty-third Psalm is David's most famous passage. In his next psalm, he made sure the reader would know why he was able to pen such beautiful words. "The earth is the Lord's, and everything in it, the world, and all who live in it" (Psalm 24:1).

God made every one of us, but He didn't create earth and all of us just so there would be a bunch of people in a pretty place. He made us with a mission in mind. He made us to glorify himself. There are many ways to glorify God. A student can do it just as wonderfully as a pastor, but it is the reason you exist.

So you are left with a choice, because God wants a loving child and not a preprogrammed microchip. You can live as a consumer or an investor. You can serve yourself, or you can serve God. This is not a *both/and* proposition. It's *either/or*, just as Jesus said in Matthew 6:24:

No one can serve two masters. Either he will hate the one and love the other, or he will be devoted to the one and despise the other.

One of the keys to God's kingdom is summarized by Jesus in Matthew 16:24. It's easier said than done, but an on-mission life—truly living the dream—comes from denying yourself, taking up your cross, and following Jesus.

This hit home for me shortly after I killed the black cat. I guess the old superstition works in reverse for snakebitten young preachers.

I was almost twenty years old when the associate pastor from First Baptist Church of Merritt Island, Florida, phoned me. I didn't know him, but he knew a mutual college friend. The pastor was looking for an intern, and the friend told him I needed some experience.

My parents were away on vacation when the pastor called me on a Saturday. I had never heard of Merritt Island. I asked him, "Well, when do you need me?"

"Actually, I needed you last Monday."

"So when do I need to be there?"

"Can you be here on Monday?"

He needed me in two days. I was still recovering from being a cat killer and wondering whether I was cut out for preaching. My parents were gone. I was home alone and unsure how to pray through the opportunity. But I spent the rest of the day opening my Bible, reading, and thinking. I was ready for something deeper, something to manifest the calling I was feeling on the inside. I was ready, finally, to jump off a cliff and see if God would catch me.

I called the pastor on Sunday afternoon and accepted the internship.

My parents pulled into the driveway later that day. I welcomed them home with hugs and then began telling them good-bye.

"Well, you'll never believe this, but this guy called and wants me as an intern in Merritt Island, Florida. I'm leaving tomorrow morning and driving eight hours to spend the summer there."

Mom's eyes widened. "You're going to do what?!"

After getting over the initial surprise, my parents were supportive of my decision. I had made the decision on my own—with God's help, of course. But I was an adult making a vital life choice. It felt good. The fact that I didn't know what the next day would hold felt even better.

I'm forty-five years old now. I still don't know what tomorrow will hold. And I've never felt better.

The decision to accept the internship changed my life because I finally let everything go and said, "Okay, Lord. I'm going to serve you. Whatever happens, whether I someday pastor a church or teach kindergarteners, I'm going to serve you."

Now, a quarter-century later, I'm still pastoring. I've often entertained the thought that there were a lot of careers I could have pursued and still honored God. I could've been an accountant and done well. I might've been a pilot. I could have followed a thousand paths, but God had a plan for my life. He had a mission for me. And though this has not been easy, it's been an unbelievable adventure.

I stayed in school until I was thirty years old to earn a doctorate. That's a lot of school and a lot of work. It hasn't always been easy, but I know one certainty. Since fully surrendering to God's calling, not once have I ever wondered, *What do I need to be doing with my life?* The reason is because early on I struggled enough and sought God enough that He convinced me, *"This is it. This is who you are. So this is what you need to be doing."*

I've been on a mission ever since, and that's one area of my life in which I have had complete resolve. In fact, when I went to seminary, I had to take a psychological profile because they wanted to determine how I would handle certain situations and where I would best fit in serving God. The exam drained me, but I remember a seminary advisor revealing my results.

"I think you graded higher than anyone has ever graded on being convinced that this is what you need to be doing," he said.

I was. I was convinced. God convinced me . . . because I sought Him.

"We can make this as hard as we want," the advisor said, "but I think that no matter how difficult it becomes, you're going to stick it out, aren't you?"

My mind raced back in time. I thought about varsity basketball and pine trees named Julius and Magic. I thought about flipping burgers, a wrecked Javelin, Billy Graham, and a blank television screen. I thought about Georgia Southern and Mercer University. I thought about a cop pulling me over on my way to telling the world that I would become a preacher. I thought about a thirteen-minute sermon and a dead cat. I thought about a tankful of gas and a map to abandonment in Merritt Island, Florida.

I thought about a hippie counselor on the beach and a voice in the stairway.

I thought about my Savior.

I smiled at the seminary advisor.

"I'm going to stick it out," I said, "because this is all I have. This is it. I have nothing to fall back on."

DREAM Resolution:

I am led to pursue a lifetime shaped by the heart of God by praying and following these steps:

_____

_____

_____

_____

I believe God's mission for me is:

_____

_____

_____

_____

_____

My personal mission statement:

_____

_____

_____

_____

_____

_____

The Secret of Life

I heard about a guy who stumbled across the secret of life in the middle of an Oklahoma coon hunt.

I'll call him Dan. He had never experienced such a hunt for raccoons—the kind you've seen in the movies in which a pack of well-trained and very loud coon hounds howl through the woods as they chase a raccoon and finally "tree" it for capture. Trailing the dogs alongside the pack's owner and trainer, Dan listened to the explanations of what was going on ahead of him. The expert could tell him which dog was baying and determine, by changes in the howls, exactly what was going on in the hunt even from thousands of yards away. Through God-given instincts and training, the dogs communicated with each other to corral the masked critter and send him scurrying up a tree.

When the raccoon was treed, the dogs broke into a different kind of yelp, one that let the approaching hunters know the quarry was cornered.

Dan was amazed. There he was, chugging along with his shotgun and flashlight, trying to follow a pack of howling dogs in the middle of the night. And it was scintillating. But it wasn't until later, back at camp, that these well-rehearsed dogs revealed their biggest surprise.

The camp cook prepared a meal as everybody celebrated a successful night. The smell of sizzling bacon teased the air as the hunters reclined and talked about the hunt. The dogs dozed in recuperation. Suddenly, the cook flung a piece of fried bacon near the pack of tuckered-out hounds.

In unison, they lurched for the strip of bacon. The dogs tore at each other, biting, jumping, head-butting, and barreling their way through the pile. Dan was shocked—not just by the ferocity of the moment but that it was happening at all.

"Man, just a little while ago, those dogs were working in perfect harmony with each other," said Dan, "and now they're at each other's throats."

The old hunter who had trained the dogs glanced at Dan with a knowing half-smile.

"That," the veteran said, "is what happens when you're not doing what you were designed for."

I've been a bit confused by the wild popularity of the Internet Web site *myspace.com*. First, I'm astounded at the willingness of so many people to lift the shades on intimate details of their lives. I've been just as stupefied at the incriminating yet eager revelations many people post on the site. It's almost as if the term "my space" lends a false sense of privacy even though it's obvious that the whole planet is only a few clicks away.

My biggest issue with the concept of "My Space" is the title, however. Man will claim ownership of almost anything, and the name of the Web site smacks of the independent nature that led to the Fall in the Garden of Eden that left mankind cursed and broken.

Ever since the devil deceived Eve into taking a bite, we all have staked out a claim, thumped our chests, and declared, "My space!" Little tykes cut to the chase. They just blare, "MINE!"

Jesus looks at your heart and declares, "My space. Mine, and mine alone."

Remember, Acts 17:28 states that we live and move and have our being in God. Do you consciously live in the presence of Almighty God? Do you live fully aware that you exist *in Him*? If not, you're missing the dream.

We may not understand it. We may not even like it. But God made us for a purpose, and He already has determined the place, out of all places on the earth, where we were born. He determined the time of our births. Why?

Why in all of time and space did He place us in the precise location we now exist?

Why? Because He has a mission for us. Right here, right now. He has a dream for us.

Living the dream is living a lifetime shaped by the heart of God. It means fulfilling the purpose for which you were created.

Matt is thirty-nine years old. I had not seen him in years, but he phoned the other day and asked to meet with me.

The first time I met him some time ago, I thought, *This is a sharp guy. He's handsome and he's healthy. He looks like an athlete. He's got a wife, a family, and a good job. Impressive.*

For a while, he was one of those folks who floated in and out of the church. Then he disappeared. Weeks turned into months before I finally heard the sad update: "Matt is about to lose everything because he's tied up in drugs."

That was about five years ago. Matt is still wrestling his demons. When Matt showed up for our meeting, his appearance had changed. He didn't look so athletic anymore. The drug lifestyle had taken its toll. Still, even among the crack-house stories, one statement lingers: "I want you to help me," Matt said. "I'm thirty-nine years old and looking at my life. One time I helped some little kids in a recreation league, and that's the only thing of any value I've ever done. I don't want to die and that be the only thing I've ever accomplished. That's pitiful. And now I'm a slave to this kind of life."

That's a heavy story. I share it because of its stark caution. Hopefully you won't wreck your life with drugs or alcohol, but I've seen many people devastated because they strayed onto the wrong path and experimented at roughly your age.

Two decades later, after swearing countless times and falsely convincing themselves that they know what they're doing and can handle it, these folks wake up to a wasted life and the realization that their only redeeming moments occurred long ago . . . moments now buried in the cobwebs of a riddled mind.

That's where Matt is now. After our recent talk, he didn't show up for our next scheduled meeting. When I finally reached him, he said, "I wasn't in any condition to come." He was strung out on drugs. Shortly afterward, he checked into a rehab center, and, as I write this, he's at a critical crossroads.

Taking such a step is frightening for an addict. Change is hard for anyone—especially for those who have been living on their own terms for years, even decades, and are slaves to their lifestyles and choices. Jesus doesn't come easy to the hardened heart. It's next to impossible to begin denying yourself at age forty when you've never done it before. There is good news, however. What is impossible for men is more than possible for Almighty God.

You have a chance to start living the dream now. Right now, today, you are setting the course for the rest of your life.

Will it be a lifetime shaped by the heart of God?

I am so thankful for my Lord and the mission He has for me.

This is my mission. I'm a pastor and a preacher.

I am a follower of Jesus Christ.

I'm not the most important pastor the world has ever witnessed. I may never lead a large crusade or speak in a sports arena. I may not pastor the most significant church in America. I may not be on nationwide television. Those incidentals don't matter. I need only to do what God has called me to do. He happened to call me to ministry, and that has helped facilitate my life's mission.

When my life nears an end, I will not look back and wonder whether I ever accomplished anything of value, because my assessment is not important. Only God's assessment matters, and I'm fulfilling His mission. *I have no doubt about that.* Therein rests such peace . . . and resolve.

I never have to wonder whether I'm doing something significant. As little as it may be—writing an article for the church bulletin, talking with a family about the problems in their home, or listening to a kid about a struggle—whatever it is, I don't have to worry whether it matters. It is significant because I'm living the dream God has for me. That's the best place to be. It's the *only* place to be. There is such a thing as God's will, and I'm living it, and it's fun.

It's a blast to be a follower of Jesus Christ.

In fact, living the dream means you live with a passion that says, "When I'm gone, the world is going to miss me. They're going to know I've been here."

That's not to say that you harbor grandiose ideas of self-importance, but it gives you a sense of value. It helps you realize that your life does make a difference. You won't walk into a pastor's office at nearly forty years old and say, "Hey, I've never done anything of value outside of working with kids one time."

A lot of people say, "You need to do something you enjoy. Too many people do stuff that they don't enjoy." Such comments can lead us astray. Many pursuits of the flesh are enjoyable for a season. No, we should do what we were *designed* to do. When we do what we're designed to do, we're going to enjoy it. It won't always be easy, but it will always be best.

So here is my parting encouragement: Pray in earnest and seek God's face to grasp His dream for you. Don't give up until He shows you.

And He *will* show you.

It doesn't mean God needs you, because He doesn't. He just wants you. Doesn't that blow your mind? He **wants** to include **you** in His mission. And as you fall in step with Him, you embark upon the grandest and freshest of journeys.

In the previous chapter, I asked you to write out your personal mission statement. I will leave you with mine. I borrowed it from a guy who stood before the elders of a local church and told them that he had to go on a dangerous mission trip. He told them they would never again see him on this earth. Paul was his name.

He was a follower of Jesus Christ.

I consider my life worth nothing to me, if only I may finish the race and complete the task the Lord Jesus has given me—the task of testifying to the gospel of God's grace. (Acts 20:24)

May it ever be.
Dream, friend. Dream big.

So, What Now?

I hope you have resolved within your heart that who you are matters far more than what you do.

Learning who you are in Christ prepares the way for you to discover what you should do with your life. But there is a high probability that even after reading this book, you are still wondering about God's purpose and plan for your life. I know all too well that can be very frustrating. But don't give up! Though we cannot "make" God give us the answers we want, we can make sure we are in the best position to hear the answers God provides. We can do some PREP work for living a life shaped by the heart of God.

What should we do?

Pray
Read
Expose
Pursue

Let's examine each important area to help you find God's direction.

Pray

I realize this may sound a bit trite, but don't overlook this aspect of your personal life in Christ. Prayer is not an elective course for the person who wants to experience and know God's heart.

Prayer isn't always about getting answers, but it *is* always about growing closer in our fellowship with God. That is one of the secrets of the Christian walk. When we get to know God's heart, we begin to grasp His desire for our lives.

Think about some of God's encouragement to talk to Him:

Then Jesus told his disciples a parable to show them that they should always pray and not give up. (Luke 18:1)

If any of you lacks wisdom, he should ask God, who gives generously to all without finding fault, and it will be given to him. But when he asks, he must believe and not doubt, because he who doubts is like a wave of the sea, blown and tossed by the wind. That man should not think he will receive anything from the Lord. (James 1:5–7)

Be joyful in hope, patient in affliction, faithful in prayer. (Romans 12:12)

If you need an example, look at the prayer life of Jesus (John 17) or be encouraged by the prayer of David, one of the writers of the Psalms:

Give ear to my words, O Lord, consider my sighing.

Listen to my cry for help, my King and my God, for to you I pray.

In the morning, O Lord, you hear my voice; in the morning I lay my requests before you and wait in expectation. (Psalm 5:1–3)

The plain truth is we need to pray. If we really want to hear from God, God needs to hear from us.

Read

Sorry. I can hear your moaning. You may not have been expecting this book to provide all the answers, but you probably didn't expect it to be the launching pad for a lifetime of reading either. But if you want to know God's heart, then you need to know God. And if you are going to know Him, you really need to read His book. The Bible can be intimidating, but it is also very interesting. Why? Because it is written from the Author of Life to those who are walking through life, so I encourage you to embrace its rich treasures.

Check out this writer's heart and perspective toward God's Word. I encourage you to position your heart to follow his:

Oh, how I love your law!
I meditate on it all day long.
Your commands make me wiser than my
    enemies,
for they are ever with me.
I have more insight than all my teachers,
for I meditate on your statutes.
I have more understanding than the elders,
for I obey your precepts.
I have kept my feet from every evil path
so that I might obey your word.
I have not departed from your laws,
for you yourself have taught me.
How sweet are your words to my taste,
sweeter than honey to my mouth!
I gain understanding from your precepts;
therefore I hate every wrong path.
Your word is a lamp to my feet
and a light for my path.
    —Psalm 119:97–105

Expose

You cannot foresee every twist and turn of your future, but I hope you now realize God has a design for all of your days.

Since we are shortsighted, it is important that we expose ourselves to environments in which we can hear from God. The best way to do this is by diving into a vibrant, biblically focused church and surrounding ourselves with people who are interested in passionately pursuing God.

I encourage you to immerse yourself in activities that inspire you to walk faithfully with God. Listen to Christian music, search the Internet for biblically sound teaching, attend Bible studies, and develop relationships with mature, godly people who are willing to mentor you. Be diligent to position yourself to hear God's voice.

One of the great challenges of discovering God's specific will for our lives is that we want to know it all and we want to know it all right now. This is where trusting God is essential. God has a plan and He is willing to reveal it to us, but usually He does this only one step at a time. Remember, "The righteous will live by faith" (Romans 1:17). So we should keep ourselves in places where we can hear God's voice.

When I was a child, I loved to play in our neighbors' yards. Mom was always quick to give me instructions for my excursions. The first rule was simple. "Make sure that wherever you go you can still hear my voice." There were times when I got distracted or was blatantly disobedient and went too far. It was in those times when I could not hear my mother's voice that I usually got into trouble.

The lesson has spiritual validity. Within your daily routine, make sure you put yourself in places and at events where you know you will hear the faithful instruction of the Bible. And always surround yourself with people who will steer you toward this goal. The Lord will use these kinds of godly environments to reveal His desires for you.

Pursue

There are many pursuits that can capture our attention and become the "thing" we live for. Pleasure, prestige, recognition, financial security, popularity, and even fun can sit in the captain's chair of our hearts.

If someone were to ask you, "What do you want most?" how would you answer? Would your response be one of the pursuits I listed or something similar? While these desires would be considered good, they are not the best. In fact, they aren't even close to the top. Many people spend their lives living for today and for themselves. This self-centered, got-to-have-it-now mentality may seem a sure way to experience happiness, but the people who have pursued it and found its end would give you a different perspective.

This assessment is even in the Bible through words penned by King Solomon:

I denied myself nothing my eyes desired; I refused my heart no pleasure. My heart took

delight in all my work, and this was the reward for all my labor. Yet when I surveyed all that my hands had done and what I had toiled to achieve, everything was meaningless, a chasing after the wind; nothing was gained under the sun.

—Ecclesiastes 2:10–11

So what pursuit should we hold dear?

Good question.

I want to encourage you to live with a transcendent purpose. Pursue a life that does not have yourself as its focal point. Live for tomorrow (eternity), not today. Live as someone who understands that we live forever. Live as someone who understands that God, the Ruler of all the universe, invites us to live in fellowship with Him and includes us in His plans. Don't be distracted or bogged down in daily demands or desires for just the ordinary. God is extraordinary. God is supernatural. There is nothing bigger or better than to live out the desires of God's heart.

Live for the One who died for you. *That* is living the dream.

endnotes

Decisions: What Time Is It?

1. C.S. Lewis, *Mere Christianity* (New York: Macmillan-Collier, 1960), 55–56.

Relationships: Giving Yourself Away

1. Adrian Rogers, *The Evolution of a Sin,* Love Worth Finding Ministries, Memphis, GE1-0739, audiocassette.

Relationships: DREAM Challenge

1. Oswald Chambers, *My Utmost for His Highest,* ed. James Reimann (Oswald Chambers Publications Association, Ltd., 1992), April 28.

Aspirations: The Seven Wills of God

1. Gregory Koukl, *Decision Making and the Will of God,* Stand to Reason, Signal Hill, Calif., 2:3, audiocassette.

acknowledgments

I am so thankful to our Lord Jesus Christ for the grace, mercy, and love He has lavished upon my life. His heart continues to shape my days and give me real joy. I would also like to acknowledge:

My parents: You always led me to the throne of God by your example and encouragement. I never could have learned more about having a servant's heart than what I learned at home. Your support and love are off the charts.

My sisters: You walked the early days of my life with me. Thanks for putting up with me! Older brothers can be a pain . . . but not me!

My grandmothers: They held Jesus out to me and now enjoy the pleasure of eternal life with the Lord they love.

My in-laws, Walt and Gerry Dejager: Your love for Jesus never ceases to teach me what it really means to live every day for Him.

The pastors of my youth: As I was growing up, you lived the dream and touched my heart. Thank you, Kenneth Holland, Dewitt Cox, and Don Ledbetter.

The awesome members of Eagle's Landing First Baptist Church: You have loved me and my family and allowed us the privilege of loving you back.

My friend and fellow staff member, Tim Luke: You took the message in my heart and made it sound "sweet." Napoleon says, "Thanks, Dude!"

The staff members of Eagle's Landing First Baptist Church: You so faithfully embody what it means to live the dream.

The students of Eagle's Landing Christian Academy: You helped to ignite the inspiration for this book, and I pray you will experience the joy of living for Jesus!

Tim Dowdy has served as senior pastor of Eagle's Landing First Baptist Church in McDonough, Georgia, since 1989. Under his leadership, the congregation has grown from a Baptist mission of thirty-nine members to a Southern Baptist church of more than four thousand. He also is president of Eagle's Landing Christian Academy, which has an enrollment of more than thirteen hundred students. Affectionately referred to as Pastor Tim, he serves on the Board of Trustees of the North American Mission Board. He is married to Christie and has one son, Micah, a student at Gordon College. This is Tim's first book.

Tim Luke serves as adult pastor at Eagle's Landing First Baptist Church. He is the coauthor of *LifeStories*, written with fellow staff member Mark Hall of the contemporary Christian band Casting Crowns. Tim joined the church staff in 2000 after serving as editor of *InTouch* magazine, the devotional magazine of Dr. Charles Stanley's ministry. The former journalist worked as a sportswriter for ten years, the last four covering the Atlanta Braves. He is married to Karen and has two sons, Jacob and J. P.